INTRODUCTION:
A PROLOGUE
FROM THE
BARD

Brave scholars, blessed with time and energy,
    At school, fair Harvard, set about to glean,
From dusty tomes and modern poetry,
    All truths and knowledge formerly unseen.
From forth the hungry minds of these good folk
    Study guides, star-floss'd, soon came to life;
Whose deep and deft analysis awoke
    The latent "A"s of those in lit'rary strife.
Aim far past passing—insight from our trove
    Will free your comprehension from its cage.
Our SparkNotes' worth, online we also prove;
    Behold this book! Same brains, but paper page.
If patient or "whatever," please attend,
    What you have missed, our toil shall strive to mend.

CONTENTS

NOTE: This SparkNote refers to *The Norton Shakespeare* edition of *1 Henry IV*. Other editions of the play may differ in line numbering, spelling, punctuation, and diction.

CONTEXT

THE MOST INFLUENTIAL WRITER in all of English literature, William Shakespeare was born in 1564 to a successful middle-class glove maker in Stratford-upon-Avon, England. Shakespeare attended grammar school, but his formal education proceeded no further. In 1582 he married an older woman, Anne Hathaway, and had three children with her. Around 1590 he left his family behind and traveled to London to work as an actor and playwright. Public and critical acclaim quickly followed, and Shakespeare eventually became the most popular playwright in England and part-owner of the Globe Theater. His career bridged the reigns of Elizabeth I (ruled 1558–1603) and James I (ruled 1603–1625), and he was a favorite of both monarchs. Indeed, James granted Shakespeare's company the greatest possible compliment by bestowing upon its members the title of King's Men. Wealthy and renowned, Shakespeare retired to Stratford and died in 1616 at the age of fifty-two. At the time of Shakespeare's death, literary luminaries such as Ben Jonson hailed his works as timeless.

Shakespeare's works were collected and printed in various editions in the century following his death, and by the early eighteenth century his reputation as the greatest poet ever to write in English was well established. The unprecedented admiration garnered by his works led to a fierce curiosity about Shakespeare's life, but the dearth of biographical information has left many details of Shakespeare's personal history shrouded in mystery. Some people have concluded from this fact and from Shakespeare's modest education that Shakespeare's plays were actually written by someone else—Francis Bacon and the Earl of Oxford are the two most popular candidates—but the support for this claim is overwhelmingly circumstantial, and the theory is not taken seriously by many scholars.

In the absence of credible evidence to the contrary, Shakespeare must be viewed as the author of the thirty-seven plays and 154 sonnets that bear his name. The legacy of this body of work is immense. A number of Shakespeare's plays seem to have transcended even the category of brilliance, becoming so influential as to affect profoundly the course of Western literature and culture ever after.

Henry IV, Part 1, more commonly referred to as *1 Henry IV*, is one of Shakespeare's history plays. It forms the second part of a tetralogy, or four-part series, that deals with the historical rise of the English royal House of Lancaster. (The tetralogy proceeds in the following order: *Richard II*, *1 Henry IV*, *2 Henry IV*—that is, *Henry IV, Part 2*—and *Henry V*.) *1 Henry IV* was probably composed in the years 1596–1597.

Set in the years 1402–1403, the action of *1 Henry IV* takes place nearly two centuries before Shakespeare's own time. In general, it follows real events and uses historical figures, although Shakespeare significantly alters or invents history where it suits him. For instance, the historical Hotspur was not the same age as Prince Harry, and Shakespeare's Mortimer is a conflation of two separate individuals. The play refers back to the history covered in *Richard II* (which can be considered its prequel), and a familiarity with the events of *Richard II* is helpful for understanding the motivations of various characters in *1 Henry IV*.

Among Shakespeare's most famous creations is Falstaff, Prince Harry's fat, aged, and criminally degenerate mentor and friend. Falstaff's irreverent wit is legendary. He has many historical precedents: he owes much to archetypes like the figure of Vice from medieval morality plays and Gluttony from medieval pageants about the seven deadly sins. His character also draws on both the *miles gloriosus* figure, an arrogant soldier from classical Greek and Roman comedy, and the Lord of Misrule, the title given an individual appointed to reign over folk festivities in medieval England. Ultimately, however, Falstaff is a Shakespearean creation, second among Shakespearean characters only to Hamlet as a subject of critical interest.

The play mixes history and comedy innovatively, moving from lofty scenes involving kings and battles to base scenes involving ruffians drinking and engaging in robberies. Its great strengths include a remarkable richness and variety of texture, a fascinatingly ambiguous take on history and on political motivations, and a new kind of characterization, as found in the inimitable Falstaff.

SHAKESPEARE'S HISTORY PLAYS: SOURCES AND CONTEXTS

Shakespeare's so-called history plays are generally thought to constitute a distinct genre. They differ somewhat in tone, form, and focus from Shakespeare's comedies, tragedies, and romances. Many of Shakespeare's other plays are set in the historical past and even treat similar themes, such as kingship and revolution—*Julius Caesar* and *Hamlet*, for instance. However, the eight works known as the history plays have several additional things in common: they form a linked series, they are set in late medieval England, and they deal with the rise and fall of the House of Lancaster (a period that later historians often referred to as the Wars of the Roses).

Shakespeare wrote his most important history plays in two tetralogies, or sequences of four plays apiece. The first series, written near the start of his career (roughly 1589–1593), consists of *1 Henry VI*, *2 Henry VI*, *3 Henry VI*, and *Richard III*, and covers the fall of the Lancaster dynasty—that is, events in English history between about 1422 and 1485. The second series, written at the height of Shakespeare's career (roughly 1595–1599), covers English history from around 1398 to 1420. This series consists of *Richard II* and the most famous history plays of all, *1 Henry IV*, *2 Henry IV*, and *Henry V*. There are two other, less-celebrated history plays: *King John*, whose title figure ruled from 1199 to 1216, and *All Is Well*, which takes the reign of Henry VIII (1509–1547) as its subject.

Although the events he writes about occurred some two centuries before his own time, Shakespeare expected his audience to be familiar with the characters and events he was describing. The battles among houses and the rise and fall of kings were woven into the cultural fabric of England and formed an integral part of the country's patriotic legends and national mythology. One might compare this knowledge to the American public's general awareness of the events and figures surrounding the American Revolution, which occurred more than two centuries ago. As it did for the English commoners of Shakespeare's era, the passage of time has obscured for us many of the specific details of important historical events, and thus the heroes and battles of an event like the American Revolution are, to some degree, cloaked in myth. Shakespearean history is similarly often inaccurate in its details, although it reflects popular conceptions of history. (A famous example is Shakespeare's portrayal of the defeated Richard III in the play of that name as an evil, malformed hunchback. Popular mythology of the time conceived of Richard as a hunchback, but little historical evidence supports the legend, and portraits from Richard's own era do not depict him as such).

Shakespeare drew on a number of sources in writing his history plays, as he did in nearly all his work. His primary source for historical material, however, is generally agreed to be the second edition of Raphael Holinshed's massive work *The Chronicles of England, Scotland and Ireland,* published in 1587. Holinshed's account provides the fundamental chronology of events that Shakespeare follows, alters, or conveniently ignores to suit his dramatic purposes. Holinshed's work was only one of an entire genre of historical chronicles, which were popular at the time. Shakespeare may well have used any number of other sources; for *Richard II,* for example, scholars have suggested at least seven possible primary sources.

An important question that preoccupies the characters in the history plays and that links these plays is whether the king of England is divinely appointed—that is, whether he is God's "deputy anointed in his sight," as John of Gaunt says in *Richard II* (I.ii.38). If such is the case, then the overthrow, deposition, or, worst of all, murder of a king is akin to blasphemy. In Shakespeare's works, as in the classical Greek tragedies (such as Aeschylus's *Oresteia*), such an act may cast a long shadow over the reign of the king who deposes or murders his predecessor, and even over his descendants. This shadow, which manifests itself in the form of literal ghosts in plays such as *Hamlet, Macbeth, Julius Caesar,* and *Richard III,* also looms over *Richard II* and its sequels. In the play that bears his name, Richard II is haunted by a politically motivated murder—not that of an actual king but that of his uncle, Thomas of Woodstock, Duke of Gloucester. After his eventual overthrow, the new king, Henry IV, is, in turn, haunted by his own responsibility for Richard's overthrow and eventual murder. This shadow hangs over both the plays that bear Henry IV's name. Only after Henry IV's death does his own son, Henry V, symbolically prove himself worthy to wear the crown and rule as king of England.

PLOT OVERVIEW

NOTE: 1 Henry IV *has two main plots that intersect in a dramatic battle at the end of the play. The first plot concerns King Henry IV, his son, Prince Harry, and their strained relationship. The second concerns a rebellion that is being plotted against King Henry by a discontented family of noblemen in the North, the Percys, who are angry because of King Henry's refusal to acknowledge his debt to them. The play's scenes alternate between these two plot strands until they come together at the play's end.*

When the play opens, military news interrupts the aging King Henry's plans to lead a crusade. The Welsh rebel Glyndŵr has defeated King Henry's army in the South, and the young Harry Percy (nicknamed Hotspur), who is supposedly loyal to King Henry, is refusing to send to the king the soldiers whom he has captured in the North. King Henry summons Hotspur back to the royal court so that he can explain his actions.

Meanwhile, King Henry's son, Prince Harry, sits drinking in a bar with criminals and highwaymen. King Henry is very disappointed in his son; it is common knowledge that Harry, the heir to the throne, conducts himself in a manner unbefitting royalty. He spends most of his time in taverns on the seedy side of London, hanging around with vagrants and other shady characters. Harry's closest friend among the crew of rascals is Falstaff, a sort of substitute father figure. Falstaff is a worldly and fat old man who steals and lies for a living. Falstaff is also an extraordinarily witty person who lives with great gusto. Harry claims that his spending time with these men is actually part of a scheme on his part to impress the public when he eventually changes his ways and adopts a more noble personality.

Falstaff's friend Poins arrives at the inn and announces that he has plotted the robbery of a group of wealthy travelers. Although Harry initially refuses to participate, Poins explains to him in private that he is actually playing a practical joke on Falstaff. Poins's plan is to hide before the robbery occurs, pretending to ditch Falstaff. After the robbery, Poins and Harry will rob Falstaff and then make fun of him when he tells the story of being robbed, which he will almost certainly fabricate.

Hotspur arrives at King Henry's court and details the reasons that his family is frustrated with the king: the Percys were instrumental in helping Henry overthrow his predecessor, but Henry has failed to repay the favor. After King Henry leaves, Hotspur's family members explain to Hotspur their plan to build an alliance to overthrow the king.

Harry and Poins, meanwhile, successfully carry out their plan to dupe Falstaff and have a great deal of fun at his expense. As they are all drinking back at the tavern, however, a messenger arrives for Harry. Harry's father has received news of the civil war that is brewing and has sent for his son; Harry is to return to the royal court the next day.

Although the Percys have gathered a formidable group of allies around them—leaders of large rebel armies from Scotland and Wales as well as powerful English nobles and clergymen who have grievances against King Henry—the alliance has begun to falter. Several key figures announce that they will not join in the effort to overthrow the king, and the danger that these defectors might alert King Henry of the rebellion necessitates going to war at once.

Heeding his father's request, Harry returns to the palace. King Henry expresses his deep sorrow and anger at his son's behavior and implies that Hotspur's valor might actually give him more right to the throne than Prince Harry's royal birth. Harry decides that it is time to reform, and he vows that he will abandon his wild ways and vanquish Hotspur in battle in order to reclaim his good name. Drafting his tavern friends to fight in King Henry's army, Harry accompanies his father to the battlefront.

The civil war is decided in a great battle at Shrewsbury. Harry boldly saves his father's life in battle and finally wins back his father's approval and affection. Harry also challenges and defeats Hotspur in single combat. King Henry's forces win, and most of the leaders of the Percy family are put to death. Falstaff manages to survive the battle by avoiding any actual fighting.

Powerful rebel forces remain in Britain, however, so King Henry must send his sons and his forces to the far reaches of his kingdom to deal with them. When the play ends, the ultimate outcome of the war has not yet been determined; one battle has been won, but another remains to be fought (Shakespeare's sequel to this play, 2 *Henry IV*, begins where *1 Henry IV* leaves off).

CHARACTER LIST

King Henry IV The ruling king of England. Henry is not actually all that old, but at the time the play opens, he has been worn down prematurely by worries. He nurses guilty feelings about having won his throne through a civil war that deposed the former king, Richard II. In addition, his reign has not brought an end to the internal strife in England, which erupts into an even bigger civil war in this play. Finally, he is vexed by the irresponsible antics of his eldest son, Prince Harry. Regal, proud, and somewhat aloof, King Henry is not the main character of the play that bears his name but, rather, its historical focus. He gives the play a center of power and a sense of stability, though his actions and emotions are largely secondary to the plot.

Prince Harry King Henry IV's son, who will eventually become King Henry V. Harry's title is Prince of Wales, but all of his friends call him Hal; he is also sometimes called Harry Monmouth. Though Harry spends all his time hanging around highwaymen, robbers, and whores, he has secret plans to transform himself into a noble prince, and his regal qualities emerge as the play unfolds. Harry is the closest thing the play has to a protagonist: his complex and impressive mind is generally at the center of the play, though Shakespeare is often somewhat ambiguous about how we are meant to understand this simultaneously deceitful and heroic young prince.

Hotspur The son and heir of the Earl of Northumberland and the nephew of the Earl of Worcester. Hotspur's real name is Henry Percy (he is also called Harry or Percy), but he has earned his nickname from his fierceness in battle and hastiness of action. Hotspur is a member of the powerful Percy family of the North, which helped bring King Henry IV to power but now feels that the king has forgotten his debt to them. In Shakespeare's account, Hotspur is the same age as Prince Harry and becomes his archrival. Quick-tempered and impatient, Hotspur is obsessed with the idea of honor and glory to the exclusion of all other qualities.

Sir John Falstaff A fat old man between the ages of about fifty and sixty-five who hangs around in taverns on the wrong side of London and makes his living as a thief, highwayman, and mooch. Falstaff is Prince Harry's closest friend and seems to act as a sort of mentor to him, instructing him in the practices of criminals and vagabonds. He is the only one of the bunch who can match Harry's quick wit pun for pun.

Earl of Westmoreland A nobleman and military leader who is a close companion and valuable ally of King Henry IV.

Lord John of Lancaster The younger son of King Henry and the younger brother of Prince Harry. John proves himself wise and valiant in battle, despite his youth.

Sir Walter Blunt A loyal and trusted ally of the king and a valuable warrior.

Thomas Percy, Earl of Worcester Hotspur's uncle. Shrewd and manipulative, Worcester is the mastermind behind the Percy rebellion.

Henry Percy, Earl of Northumberland Hotspur's father. Northumberland conspires and raises troops on the Percy side, but he claims that he is sick before the Battle of Shrewsbury and does not actually bring his troops into the fray.

Edmund Mortimer, called the Earl of March The Welsh rebel Owain Glyndŵr's son-in-law. Mortimer is a conflation of two separate historical figures: Mortimer and the Earl of March. For Shakespeare's purposes, Mortimer matters because he had a strong claim to the throne of England before King Henry overthrew the previous king, Richard II.

Owain Glyndŵr The leader of the Welsh rebels and the father of Lady Mortimer (most editions of *1 Henry IV* refer to him as Owen Glendower). Glyndŵr joins with the Percys in their insurrection against King Henry. Well-read, educated in England, and very capable in battle, he is also steeped in the traditional lore of Wales and claims to be able to command great magic. He is mysterious and superstitious and sometimes acts according to prophecies and omens.

Archibald, Earl of Douglas The leader of the large army of Scottish rebels against King Henry. Usually called "The Douglas" (a traditional way of referring to a Scottish clan chief), the deadly and fearless Douglas fights on the side of the Percys.

Sir Richard Vernon A relative and ally of the Earl of Worcester.

The Archbishop of York The archbishop, whose given name is Richard Scrope, has a grievance against King Henry and thus conspires on the side of the Percys.

Ned Poins, Bardolph, and Peto Criminals and highwaymen. Poins, Bardolph, and Peto are friends of Falstaff and Prince Harry who drink with them in the Boar's Head Tavern, accompany them in highway robbery, and go with them to war.

Gadshill Another highwayman friend of Harry, Falstaff, and the rest. Gadshill seems to be nicknamed after the place on the London road—called Gad's Hill—where he has set up many robberies.

Mistress Quickly Hostess of the Boar's Head Tavern, a seedy dive in Eastcheap, London, where Falstaff and his friends go to drink.

ANALYSIS OF MAJOR CHARACTERS

PRINCE HARRY

The complex Prince Harry is at the center of events in *1 Henry IV*. As the only character to move between the grave, serious world of King Henry and Hotspur and the rollicking, comical world of Falstaff and the Boar's Head Tavern, Harry serves as a bridge uniting the play's two major plotlines. An initially disreputable prince who eventually wins back his honor and the king's esteem, Harry undergoes the greatest dramatic development in the play, deliberately transforming himself from the wastrel he pretends to be into a noble leader. Additionally, as the character whose sense of honor and leadership Shakespeare most directly endorses, Harry is, at least by implication, the moral focus of the play.

Harry is nevertheless a complicated character and one whose real nature is very difficult to pin down. As the play opens, Harry has been idling away his time with Falstaff and earning the displeasure of both his father and England as a whole. He then surprises everyone by declaring that his dissolute lifestyle is all an act: he is simply trying to lower the expectations that surround him so that, when he must, he can emerge as his true, heroic self, shock the whole country, and win the people's love and his father's admiration. Harry is clearly intelligent and already capable of the psychological machinations required of kings.

But the heavy measure of deceit involved in his plan seems to call his honor into question, and his treatment of Falstaff further sullies his name: though there seems to be real affection between the prince and the roguish knight, Harry is quite capable of tormenting and humiliating his friend (and, when he becomes king in *2 Henry IV*, of disowning him altogether). Shakespeare seems to include these aspects of Harry's character in order to illustrate that Falstaff's selfish bragging does not fool Harry and to show that Harry is capable of making the difficult personal choices that a king must make in order to rule a nation well. In any case, Harry's emergence here as a heroic young prince is probably *1 Henry IV*'s defining dynamic, and it opens the door for Prince Harry to become the great King Henry V in the next two plays in Shakespeare's sequence.

SIR JOHN FALSTAFF

Old, fat, lazy, selfish, dishonest, corrupt, thieving, manipulative, boastful, and lecherous, Falstaff is, despite his many negative qualities, perhaps the most popular of all of Shakespeare's comic characters. Though he is technically a knight, Falstaff's lifestyle clearly renders him incompatible with the ideals of courtly chivalry that one typically associates with knighthood. For instance, Falstaff is willing to commit robbery for the money and entertainment of it. As Falstaff himself notes at some length, honor is useless to him: "Can honour set-to a leg? No. Or an arm? No. Or take away the grief of a wound? No. . . . What is honour? A word" (V.i.130–133). He perceives honor as a mere "word," an abstract concept that has no relevance to practical matters. Nevertheless, though Falstaff mocks honor by linking it to violence, to which it is intimately connected throughout the play, he remains endearing and likable to Shakespeare's audiences. Two reasons that Falstaff retains this esteem are that he plays his scoundrel's role with such gusto and that he never enjoys enough success to become a real villain; even his highway robbery ends in humiliation for him.

Falstaff seems to scorn morality largely because he has such a hearty appetite for life and finds the niceties of courtesy and honor useless when there are jokes to be told and feasts to be eaten. Largely a creature of words, Falstaff has earned the admiration of some Shakespearean scholars because of the self-creation he achieves through language: Falstaff is constantly creating a myth of Falstaff, and this myth defines his identity even when it is visibly revealed to be false. A master of punning and wordplay, Falstaff provides most of the comedy in the play (just as he does in 2 *Henry IV, The Merry Wives of Windsor,* and *Henry V*). He redeems himself largely through his real affection for Prince Harry, whom, despite everything, he seems to regard as a real friend. This affection makes Harry's decision, foreshadowed in 1 *Henry IV,* to abandon Falstaff when he becomes king (in 2 *Henry IV*) seem all the more harsh.

KING HENRY IV

The title character of *1 Henry IV* appears in *Richard II* as the ambitious, energetic, and capable Bolingbroke, who seizes the throne from the inept Richard II after likely arranging his murder. Though Henry is not yet truly an old man in *1 Henry IV*, his worries about his crumbling kingdom, guilt over his uprising against Richard II, and the vagaries of his son's behavior have diluted his earlier energy and strength. Henry remains stern, aloof, and resolute, but he is no longer the force of nature he appears to be in *Richard II*. Henry's trouble stems from his own uneasy conscience and his uncertainty about the legitimacy of his rule. After all, he himself is a murderer who has illegally usurped the throne from Richard II. Therefore, it is difficult to blame Hotspur and the Percys for wanting to usurp his throne for themselves. Furthermore, it is unclear how Henry's kingship is any more legitimate than that of Richard II. Henry thus lacks the moral legitimacy that every effective ruler needs.

With these concerns lurking at the back of his reign, Henry is unable to rule as the magnificent leader his son Harry will become. Throughout the play he retains his tight, tenuous hold on the throne, and he never loses his majesty. But with an ethical sense clouded by his own sense of compromised honor, it is clear that Henry can never be a great king or anything more than a caretaker to the throne that awaits Henry V.

CHARACTER ANALYSIS

Themes, Motifs & Symbols

Themes

Themes are the fundamental and often universal ideas explored in a literary work.

The Nature of Honor

Though it is one of the principal themes of the play, the concept of honor is never given a consistent definition in *1 Henry IV*. In fact, the very multiplicity of views on honor that Shakespeare explores suggests that, in the end, honor is merely a lofty reflection of an individual's personality and conscience. In other words, honor seems to be defined less by an overarching set of guidelines and more by an individual's personal values and goals. Thus runs the argument of Hotspur, a quick-tempered and military-minded young man. He feels that honor has to do with glory on the battlefield and with defending one's reputation and good name against any perceived insult. For the troubled and contemplative King Henry IV, on the other hand, honor has to do with the well-being of the nation and the legitimacy of its ruler. One of the reasons Henry is troubled is that he perceives his own rebellion against Richard II, which won him the crown, to be a dishonorable act.

For the complex Prince Harry, honor seems to be associated with noble behavior, but for long stretches of time Harry is willing to sacrifice the appearance of honor for the sake of his own goals, confident that he can regain his honor at will. Harry's conception of honor is so all-inclusive that he believes that, by killing Hotspur, Hotspur's honor becomes his own. For the amoral rogue Falstaff, the whole idea of honor is nothing but hot air and wasted effort that does no one any good. All the major characters in the play are concerned with honor, but their opinions about the subject illuminate more about them than they do about the concept of honor.

THE LEGITIMACY OF RULERSHIP

Because *1 Henry IV* is set amid political instability and violent rebellion, the play is naturally concerned with the idea of rulership. It questions what makes a ruler legitimate, which qualities are desirable in a ruler, when it is acceptable to usurp a ruler's authority, and what the consequences of rebelling against a ruler might be. The concept of legitimate rule is deeply connected in the play with the concept of rebellion: if a ruler is illegitimate, then it is acceptable to usurp his power, as Hotspur and the Percys attempt to do with King Henry. While the criteria that make a ruler legitimate differ—legitimate rule may be attributed to the will of the people or to the will of God—on some level the crack in Henry's power results from his own fear that his rule is illegitimate, since he illegally usurped the crown from Richard II.

The consequences of failed rulership are explored in the scenes depicting the violence of lawlessness and rebellion sweeping England—the robbery in Act II, the battle in Act V, and so forth. The qualities that are desirable in a ruler are explored through the contrast inherent in the play's major characters: the stern and aloof Henry, the unpredictable and intelligent Harry, and the decisive and hot-tempered Hotspur. Each man offers a very different style of rulership. In the end, Shakespeare seems to endorse Harry's ability to think his way through a situation and to manipulate others without straying too far from the dictates of conscience. In any event, Harry emerges as Shakespeare's most impressive English king two plays later, in *Henry V*.

HIGH AND LOW LANGUAGE

One of the characteristics that sets *1 Henry IV* apart from many of Shakespeare's other plays is the ease with which it transitions between scenes populated by nobility and scenes populated by commoners. One result of these transitions is that the play encompasses many different languages and manners of expression. From the Welsh and Irish not understood by the English characters to the bartenders' coarse language Harry picks up and uses to insinuate himself in their society, these languages display the extremely diverse cast of characters that populates Shakespeare's stage.

But even more significant is the fact that knowledge of these languages and the ability to transition between them proves to be an invaluable tool. Harry makes friends quickly with the bartenders precisely because, unlike his father, he is able to emulate them and speak their language, leaving courtly diction behind. Harry demonstrates that he is not restricted to only one kind of language when he eloquently declares his loyalty to his father; his ability to speak to commoners and kings alike gives him a great deal of power.

Although language is seldom discussed by the characters in *1 Henry IV*, the sheer variety of spoken language in the play suggests that one of Shakespeare's aims with this work was to portray something of the scope of the English language. In addition to high speech and low speech, there is poetry and prose, as well as the various accents of Britain's various locales. The varied nature of the play's language suits the multiplicity of its settings. Shakespeare shows that he can capture the speech of common thieves on a dark night, warriors on the way to battle, and courtiers in the royal palace. Shakespeare utilizes various rhetorical and formal strategies to distinguish his various types of speech without sacrificing his unifying style: generally, for instance, well-born characters tend to speak in verse, while commoners tend to speak in prose.

MOTIFS

Motifs are recurring structures, contrasts, or literary devices that can help to develop and inform the text's major themes.

DOUBLES

1 Henry IV explores many different sides of a few major themes. Its primary technique for this multifaceted exploration is one of simple contrast. The differences between Harry and Hotspur make a statement on different perceptions of honor, just as the differences between the Boar's Head Tavern and the royal palace make a statement on the breadth of England's class differences. In utilizing contrast as a major thematic device, the play creates a motif of doubles, in which characters, actions, and scenes are often repeated in varied form throughout the play. For instance, Falstaff and the king act as doubles in that both are father figures for Harry. Harry and Hotspur act as doubles in that both are potential successors to Henry IV. Falstaff's comical robbery in Act II, scene ii serves as a kind of lower-class double to the nobles' Battle of Shrewsbury, exploring the consequences of rebellion against the law.

BRITISH CULTURES

As befits the play's general multiplicity of ideas, Shakespeare is preoccupied throughout much of *1 Henry IV* with the contrasts and relationships of the different cultures native to the British Isles and united under the rule of the king. Accents, folk traditions, and geographies are discussed and analyzed, particularly through the use of Welsh characters such as Glyndŵr and Scottish characters such as the Douglas. Shakespeare also rehearses the various stereotypes surrounding each character type, portraying Glyndŵr as an ominous magician and the Douglas as a hotheaded warrior.

MAGIC

A strong current of magic runs throughout the play, which is primarily a result of the inclusion of the wizardly Glyndŵr. Magic has very little to do with the plot, but it is discussed by different characters with uncommon frequency throughout the play. As with the subject of honor, a character's opinion about the existence of magic tends to say more about the character than it does about the subject itself. The pragmatic and overconfident Hotspur, for instance, expresses contempt for belief in the black arts, repeatedly mocking Glyndŵr for claiming to have magical powers. The sensuous and narcissistic Glyndŵr, by contrast, seems to give full credence to the idea of magic and to the idea that he is a magician—credence that says more about Glyndŵr's own propensity for self-aggrandizement than about the reality of magic itself.

SYMBOLS

Symbols are objects, characters, figures, or colors used to represent abstract ideas or concepts.

REPRESENTATIVE CHARACTERS

Like most of Shakespeare's other history plays, *1 Henry IV* does not make great use of symbolism as a literary device: the play concerns real people and events and so tells a much more concrete story than a more symbolic play like *Macbeth* or *The Tempest*. The most important symbols, generally speaking, are the characters themselves, and what they represent is simply the set of ideas and traits with which they are involved. Glyndŵr represents both the Welsh motif in the play and the motif of magic, while Hotspur represents rebellion and the idea that honor is won and lost in battle.

THE SUN

The sun in *1 Henry IV* represents the king and his reign. Both Harry and his father, Henry, use an image of the sun obscured by clouds to describe themselves—the former in Act I, scene ii, lines 175–181, and the latter in Act III, scene ii, lines 79–84. For King Henry, the clouds that blur his light come from his own doubts about the legitimacy of his reign. For Harry, these clouds are the shades of his immaturity and initial refusal to accept and adopt his noble responsibilities. Having accepted his royal duties, Harry can anticipate shining through these clouds and radiating his full regal glory.

SYMBOLS

Summary & Analysis

Act I, scene i

Summary

> *I . . .*
> *See riot and dishonor stain the brow*
> *Of my young Harry.*   (See QUOTATIONS, p. 57)

In the royal palace of London, King Henry IV of England speaks with his counselors. Worn out by the recent civil wars that have wracked his country, Henry looks forward to a project he has been planning for a long time: joining in the Crusades. He plans to lead a military expedition to Jerusalem, the Holy Land, to join in the battle between the Islamic peoples who currently occupy it and the European armies who are trying to seize it for the sake of Christianity.

However, news from two separate borders of Henry's kingdom almost immediately changes his plans: skirmishes have broken out between the English forces on one side and Scottish and Welsh rebels on the other. The king's trusted advisor, the Earl of Westmoreland, relays the bad news that Edmund Mortimer, an English military leader, has lost a battle against a band of guerrilla fighters in Wales, who are led by the powerful and mysterious Welsh rebel Owain Glyndŵr. Glyndŵr has captured Mortimer, and the rebels have slaughtered one thousand of Mortimer's soldiers. Moreover, the Welsh women, following their traditions, have mutilated the soldiers' corpses.

From the other English border, Westmoreland adds, he has just received information that young Harry Percy, nicknamed Hotspur, another of the king's best military men, is currently engaged in heated battle with Archibald, also known as the Douglas, the leader of a large band of Scottish rebels. King Henry has been previously told about this development, it turns out, and already possesses an update about the outcome: young Hotspur has defeated the Douglas and his army of ten thousand and has taken prisoner several important figures among the Scotsmen, including the Douglas's own son Mordake, Earl of Fife. King Henry is pleased at the news and cannot help comparing Hotspur's achievements with the idleness of his son, Prince Harry: Harry is the same age as Hotspur, but he has not won any military glory. Indeed, Harry's dishonorable behavior makes King Henry ashamed; he wishes that Hotspur were his son instead.

Hotspur, however, is behaving very strangely: he has sent word to King Henry that he plans to send only one of his prisoners (Mordake) to the king and retain the rest. This action flouts standard procedure, as the king has an automatic right to all noble prisoners captured in battle. Westmoreland suggests that Hotspur's rebellious act comes at the prompting of his uncle, the Earl of Worcester, who is known to be hostile to the king. The angered Henry concurs and says that he has sent for Hotspur, demanding that he come and explain himself. Henry decides that the Crusades project will have to be put off and that he will hold court the next Wednesday at Windsor Castle to hear what Hotspur has to say.

ANALYSIS

The plot of *1 Henry IV* is an outgrowth of dramatic historical events from England's past. King Henry's opening remark that "[t]hose opposèd eyes / Which . . . / . . . / Did lately meet in the intestine shock / And furious close of civil butchery" will no longer spill English blood on English soil refers to the recent power struggle between various English nobles (I.i.9–13). Shakespeare would have expected his audience to know the events to which Henry refers. Indeed, Shakespeare himself had dramatized them in one of his earlier plays, *Richard II*: as a result of a civil war in England, Henry managed to win the crown from Richard II, the previous king. Henry is now haunted by the violence that he used to gain the crown, and he must fight another civil war to stay in power.

Henry is already worn down by a vague sense of guilt and by uneasiness about the legitimacy of his seat on the throne. Henry has blood on his hands, since he had Richard murdered after overthrowing him. Henry bears himself regally, but he is so concerned about the recent unrest in his country that he is "shaken" and "wan with care," or pale with worry (I.i.1). Although he is not very old at the play's opening, life has already fatigued him noticeably.

Through other characters' discussions, this scene also introduces Hotspur, a young man the same age as Prince Harry and something of a foil (a character whose emotions or attitudes contrast with, and thereby accentuate, those of another character) for him. Though they have the same given name (Henry), Hotspur and Harry are as different as night and day. Hotspur is bold, quick-tempered, and loves battle; Westmoreland and King Henry talk about his remarkable accomplishment in defeating the Earl of Douglas. Harry, on the other hand, appears to be lazy, cowardly, and self-indulgent.

The comparison that King Henry makes between Hotspur and Harry is the first of many such comparisons that occur as the balance of power and honor shifts between the two young men. King Henry believes that Hotspur is "the theme of honour's tongue" but that "riot and dishonour stain the brow / Of my young Harry," that is, Prince Harry (I.i.80–84). Henry even wishes that Hotspur were his real son, since Hotspur is the one who seems to behave in a truly princely fashion. Harry eventually realizes the value of Hotspur's qualities too, and he strives to match and surpass them as he grows into his princely role.

Finally, the scene introduces us to some of the interesting cast of characters who later fight against Henry's forces. Some of these figures are not English at all but instead lead native rebel bands from the countries bordering England, over which English rulers hold only tenuous control. Reports are made of the fearless Archibald, Earl of Douglas, a powerful Scottish leader who fought Hotspur near the northern border of England. Also discussed is "the irregular and wild" Owain Glyndŵr, leader of a band of native guerrilla fighters in Wales (I.i.40). The English associate Glyndŵr with the mysterious, dark sorcery native to Wales and conceive of him as a magician. The "beastly shameless transformation" that the Welsh women perform upon the bodies of the dead Englishmen—presumably a ritual castration or a related rite—is thought to be a kind of voodoo or mysterious native magic (I.i.42–46). This sort of nervous interest in the oppressed native cultures of Britain is a running motif throughout the play.

SUMMARY & ANALYSIS

ACT I, SCENE II

SUMMARY

> *So, when this loose behaviour I throw off*
> *. . .My reformation . . .*
> *Shall show more goodly. . . .* (See QUOTATIONS, p. 58)

In his dwelling somewhere in London, Prince Harry passes the time with his friend Sir John Falstaff. Falstaff is an old, fat criminal who loves to drink sack (sweet wine), eat, and sleep away the day. He makes his living as a highwayman and robber and sponges off Harry and his other friends. But Falstaff is clever and entertaining, and he and Harry exchange familiar banter and quick-witted puns.

Harry and Falstaff are joined by their acquaintance Edward ("Ned") Poins, who is also a highwayman. Poins tells them that a robbery has been set up for early the following morning. He and Gadshill, another thief, have learned that some rich pilgrims and prosperous traders will be passing Gad's Hill (a place on the London road famous for its robberies) at around four o'clock in the morning. Falstaff says that he will participate in the robbery, and he urges Harry to come along too. Harry refuses, saying that he is not a thief, but Poins asks Falstaff to leave him alone with Harry, suggesting that he will be able to persuade the prince to go with them.

When they are alone, Poins explains to Harry that he has a marvelous practical joke planned: Poins and Harry will ride out to Gad's Hill with their four friends during the night, but they will pretend to get lost and not show up at the meeting place. Instead, they will hide and watch as the robbery occurs. Then, Poins and Harry will rob Falstaff and the others, taking the money that their friends have just stolen. Poins assures Harry that he has masks to hide their faces and suits of rough cloth ("buckram") to hide their clothes (I.ii.159). He also points out that since Falstaff and the others are complete cowards, they are sure to run away as soon as Poins and Harry attack them. The best part of the trick will be listening to the enormous lies that Falstaff is sure to tell about the encounter. At this point, Poins and Harry will be able to cut him down when they reveal that they themselves were the thieves. Amused, Harry agrees to play along.

As soon as Poins leaves the room, however, Harry begins to muse aloud to himself. He reveals that he hangs around with these low-class friends as part of a clever psychological plan: he is deliberately trying to make his father and the English people think poorly of him so that he can surprise and impress them all when he decides to grow up and start behaving like a royal prince. Harry feels that if he lowers people's expectations of him, it will be much easier to awe and please them later on than it would be if people expected great things of him. Thus, he deliberately chooses friends and a lifestyle that he knows will disappoint his father and the populace. Harry concludes by suggesting that sometime very soon he plans to reveal his true nature to those around him.

ANALYSIS

Act I, scene ii is of considerable importance because it introduces one of Shakespeare's most famous and beloved characters: Harry's friend and mentor Falstaff. The Shakespearean critic Harold Bloom says of him that "no other literary character . . . seems to me so infinite in provoking thought and in arousing emotion." This assessment may seem surprising since, after all, Falstaff is presented as a zany, antiquated criminal who does nothing but make outrageous puns. But Falstaff develops throughout the rest of this play and its sequel into something quite unusual: a cheerful, unembarrassed, self-confident lowlife whose value system runs counter to that of all the noblemen and kings who figure in the main plot of the play.

On the one hand, Falstaff is obviously a criminal, as all his banter about judges and hanging and his extravagant references to himself and other highwaymen as "squires of the night's body"—nocturnal thieves—suggest (I.ii.21). More than that, however, Falstaff seems to live with a sense of gusto and enjoyment that is completely foreign to royalty. His approach to life and honor and the way he regards himself are very different from the rigid and complicated systems of pride and vengeance that cause the noblemen to fight bloody wars and attempt to overthrow kings.

Critics are intrigued by the complexity of Falstaff's character: Falstaff is an opportunist, always turning a situation to his own advantage and usually not hesitating to step on other people as he does it. On the other hand, he seems to have no need for revenge— the lack of which differentiates him from the noblemen, including Harry. Falstaff does not hesitate to lie outrageously, but he is not concerned when he is caught. He sees no value in gaining honor by risking his life but instead believes he can find more honor in keeping his life. In short, Falstaff is interested in his own self-preservation and in living and enjoying his life to the fullest. As Bloom states: "All the self-contradictions of [Falstaff's] complex nature resolve themselves in his exuberance of being, his passion for being alive. Many of us become machines for fulfilling responsibilities; Falstaff is the largest and best reproach we can find." Alongside the principal plot of kings and earls doing battle for the fate of a nation, Falstaff constantly provides a counterpoint to their logic and values.

The relationship between Falstaff and Harry is complex. Falstaff seems to be fond of Harry, but it is strange that Harry enjoys spending time with Falstaff. This introductory scene demonstrates the apparently good-natured, joking sort of relationship that exists between them. But as Falstaff's extraordinary facility with language and knowledge of the seedy underbelly of London come to light, it becomes clear that Harry is also learning from Falstaff. The older man is, in a sense, instructing Harry in a robust way of life quite outside the noble sphere—the life that Falstaff himself leads and the philosophy that governs it.

Harry's unexpected monologue at the end of the scene reveals the complexity of his character. In stating that he will shock others' expectations "[b]y how much better than my word I am," Harry establishes a dichotomy between what his deeds compel others to think he is like and what he is actually like (I.ii.188). He thus enjoys, and is aware that he enjoys, a certain power over others by being able to control how they perceive him. His belief that "[m]y reformation, glitt'ring o'er my fault, / Shall show more goodly . . . / Than that which hath no foil to set it off" reflects the absolute deliberateness of his actions (I.ii.191–193). He sets himself up as his own "foil" in order to accentuate the seeming near miracle of his eventual transformation from lowliness to nobility.

This monologue also emphasizes Harry's plan to cast off his ruffian friends in order to cut a more impressive figure in the eyes of the world. But Harry's plan is morally ambiguous. On the one hand, it is a movement toward the honorable conduct that his father and the other noblemen want for him, but, on the other, it is extremely deceitful. Harry is now concealing the truth from everyone—his current friends, his father, and the English people.

ACT I, SCENE III

SUMMARY

I then, all smarting with my wounds being cold —
To be so pestered with a popinjay! —.

(See QUOTATIONS, p. 59)

Hotspur has answered the summons of King Henry and has come to see him at Windsor Castle in order to explain his refusal to hand over the prisoners he captured in Scotland. Hotspur's father, the Earl of Northumberland, and his uncle, the Earl of Worcester, accompany him.

Henry, angry at Hotspur's rebellious refusal to deliver the prisoners to him, speaks to Hotspur in threatening language. When Worcester, already hostile toward Henry, reacts rudely, Henry orders him out of the room. Hotspur and Northumberland now try to explain that Hotspur's refusal to return the captives was not meant as an act of rebellion. The very moment that Hotspur's battle against the Scots ended, it seems, a prissy and effeminate courtier arrived with Henry's demands for the prisoners. Wounded, tired, and angry, Hotspur refused and insulted the foolish messenger in the heat of the moment.

But Henry's anger is not soothed. Hotspur still refuses to hand over the prisoners—unless the king pays the ransom that the Welsh rebels demand for the release of Hotspur's brother-in-law, Lord Mortimer, who was captured after the Welsh defeated his army. Henry refuses, calling Mortimer a traitor. He has learned that Mortimer recently married the daughter of the Welsh rebel Glyndŵr and believes that Mortimer lost his battle with Glyndŵr on purpose. Hotspur denies this charge against his kinsman, but Henry calls him a liar. He forbids Hotspur to mention Mortimer's name ever again and demands he return the prisoners instantly or face retribution.

After Henry and his attendants leave the room, Worcester returns to his brother and nephew, and Hotspur unleashes an enraged speech. He alleges that Henry may have ulterior motives for refusing to ransom Mortimer: before he was deposed, Richard II, Henry's predecessor, had named Mortimer heir to the throne. Since Henry obtained his crown by deposing Richard illegally, Mortimer's claim to the kingdom might be better than Henry's own. Hotspur is also bitter because his own family members helped

Henry overthrow Richard in the first place, and they were instrumental in Henry's rise to power. Hotspur is thus angry that Henry seems to have forgotten the debt he owes to the Percy family.

Worcester and Northumberland have some trouble getting Hotspur to quiet down, but finally Worcester succeeds in explaining that he has already formulated a cunning (and complicated) plan. He says that the Percys must seek an alliance with the rebel forces in both Scotland and Wales and all the powerful English nobles who are dissatisfied with Henry. For now, Hotspur is to return to Scotland, give all his prisoners back to their people without demanding ransom, and establish an alliance with the Douglas, the leader of the Scottish rebellion. Northumberland is to seek the support of the Archbishop of York, who is unhappy because Henry executed his brother for conspiring against the king's life. Worcester, meanwhile, will go to Wales to discuss strategy with Mortimer and Glyndŵr.

ANALYSIS

Hotspur's dialogue in this scene is typical of his speeches throughout the play: he is a very eloquent speaker and can use words powerfully, but he has a hard time keeping his temper and is always interrupting others. The difficulty Northumberland and Worcester have in getting him to be quiet so that they can discuss their conspiracy indicates that Hotspur's impatience, which helps win him glory on the battlefield, may cause him difficulty in his personal interactions. It also suggests that while he is a brave fighter, he is a bad strategist, since his rashness makes him prone to alienate even his own allies.

Hotspur's military, aggressive, masculine nature is behind his contempt for the effeminate messenger who chattered at Hotspur like a "popinjay" after Hotspur's victory (I.iii.49). Based on the account that he gives to Henry, it seems that Hotspur reacted to the prissy courtier not only with scorn but also with an unreasonable anger (since he is using his reaction to the messenger as an excuse, however, he may be exaggerating the extent of his anger). In line with his soldierly existence, Hotspur is highly concerned with honor, which he demonstrates in his rants about his eagerness to face down Henry. His often-quoted words

SUMMARY & ANALYSIS

> By heaven, methinks it were an easy leap
> To pluck bright honour from the pale-faced moon,
> Or dive into the bottom of the deep,
>   . . .
> And pluck up drownèd honour by the locks
>   (I.iii.199–203)

emphasize not only that he is perpetually ready to face any danger in pursuit of glory but also that he has a very tangible conception of honor. Whereas Falstaff sees honor only as an abstract and therefore useless entity ("What is honour? A word. What is in that word 'honour'? . . . Air" [V.i.133–134]), Hotspur sees it as a physical object to be "pluck[ed] up," a buried treasure at "the bottom of the deep."

But a comment by Worcester suggests the shallowness of this value system. Realizing that Hotspur is not paying attention to the important plan he is trying to explain, Worcester says of Hotspur: "He apprehends a world of figures here, / But not the form of what he should attend" (I.iii.207–208). Hotspur's tendency to chase after ideals instead of thinking practically is a serious flaw in his ability to perform as a strategist and soldier. Harry, in contrast, possesses the ability to hold back and think things through, as he demonstrates in his manipulation of his tavern friends.

This scene also provides a window into the moral ambiguities at the center of the play. Many readers and critics feel that there is no clear-cut good or bad side in this and the other Henry plays. It remains ambiguous whether the Percys have a legitimate grievance, or if the king is right in dismissing their claims as the excuses of power-hungry rebels. Even the bare facts behind the coalitions are difficult or impossible to confirm. To some extent, the setup of the play urges identification with the side in power (King Henry and his allies). But the richness of the play derives from the ambiguous and mixed motives that drive its action and so many of its characters.

ACT II, SCENES I–III

SUMMARY: ACT II, SCENE I

At an inn yard in Rochester, beside the main highway about twenty-five miles outside of London, two carriers—middlemen who deliver goods from one merchant to another—are readying their horses to depart in the early-morning darkness. The stableboy is slow in coming out to help, and the carriers are annoyed. Gadshill, the highwayman friend of Falstaff and Harry, appears out of the darkness and asks the carriers if he may borrow a lantern. They are suspicious of Gadshill, however, and refuse.

As soon as the carriers have gone on their way, a chamberlain of the inn comes out to talk to Gadshill; he is Gadshill's informer. He tells him that some very wealthy travelers are currently having their breakfast in the inn and will be on the road soon. Gadshill offers him a cut of the profits, which the chamberlain refuses. Gadshill then calls for his horse and rides off to set his ambush.

SUMMARY: ACT II, SCENE II
Waiting a few miles further along the highway, at Gad's Hill, Falstaff searches for his horse—Poins has secretly taken it from where it was tied and concealed it in the woods. Peto, Bardolph, and Harry, who is in on the joke, stand by. The fat Falstaff is very uncomfortable on foot and, puffing and panting, complains loudly. Harry soothes Falstaff by telling him he will look for his horse (which, of course, he does not intend to do).

Gadshill shows up to complete the party with the news that the wealthy travelers are approaching. Harry suggests that Falstaff, Peto, Bardolph, and Gadshill confront the travelers on the highway; Harry and Poins will then flank them on either side of the road to catch any who try to escape. The men put on their masks, and Poins and Harry disappear into hiding. The travelers appear, and Falstaff, Peto, Bardolph, and Gadshill rob them and tie them up.

SUMMARY: ACT II, SCENE III
As the four split up the gold, Poins and Harry, in their buckram disguises and new masks, charge the thieves and demand their money. The four flee in terror without putting up a fight—only Falstaff even tries to get in a blow or two. Laden with gold and mightily entertained, Poins and Harry go to their horses, laughing to think of how angry Falstaff will be when he finds out that they have gotten rid of his horse and that he will have to walk back to London.

ANALYSIS: ACT II, SCENES I–III
1 Henry IV covers a wide range of terrain, both in terms of the literal geography of England and in terms of the classes of people in the

play. Shakespeare interweaves *high* scenes, which feature noblemen engaging in debates about the nature of kingship or the strategies of war, with *low* scenes of commoners and criminals engaged in various petty plots. This combination was something fairly new for Shakespeare and for English drama as a whole, causing critics and readers alike to compare the play to Geoffrey Chaucer's great Middle English work, *The Canterbury Tales,* written at the end of the fourteenth century.

Scenes i through iii of Act II offer good examples of this contrast. Here Shakespeare moves beyond his frequently used locale of the Boar's Head Tavern to conjure up the front yards of cheap roadside inns and the highway ambushes of dangerous—if bungling and cowardly—robbers. The robbery scene, with its lawlessness and violence, offers a *low* parallel to the *high* rebellion of the Percys later in the play and thus acts as both a mirror and a subtle instance of foreshadowing, hinting at the rapid disintegration of stability and peace in England.

The carriers' conversation (which, although lively, is almost unintelligible to contemporary readers without annotations) is an example of the sort of lower-class voice not usually found in the history plays of Shakespeare's contemporaries. It also provides an example of the wide range of different dialects and modes of speech that Shakespeare presents throughout the play. These range from the noble language of the royal characters and the wittiness of Falstaff to the foreign accents of Glyndŵr and the Douglas and the uneducated but lively voices of the robbers and the tavern hostess. The sheer diversity of speech in *1 Henry IV* suggests a preoccupation with the richness and multiplicity of the English language as it is manifested in various social and cultural forms.

The practical joke that Poins and Harry play on Falstaff, Bardolph, Peto, and Gadshill, while amusing, further complicates the friendship between Harry and Falstaff. Harry seems to have no problem insulting Falstaff far more viciously than Falstaff ever insults him. Similarly, he doesn't mind causing Falstaff discomfort, as when he and Poins steal his horse and force him to walk back to London. As Falstaff himself puts it, "Eight yards of uneven ground is threescore and ten [i.e., seventy] miles afoot with me, and the stony-hearted villains know it well enough" (II.ii.23–26). The ultimate point of the joke, moreover, is to humiliate Falstaff by catching him in the lie that Harry and Poins know he will tell about the affair. Harry's attitude toward his friend and mentor is uneven: he often treats Falstaff affectionately, but he can also be sadistic. This ambivalence becomes increasingly important during this play and its sequel, 2 *Henry IV*.

The joke also raises questions about whether Harry can regain the all-important honor that he has lost by behaving badly—the same honor that Hotspur currently holds in the eyes of the populace and the king. This quest for honor becomes the central point of contention between Harry and his rival; as Shakespeare likes to make mirrors of important scenes and ideas, reflecting among the lowlifes what occurs among the nobility, a concern for honor shows up among the play's lowlifes as well. Poins and Harry's betrayal of the other highwaymen supports the old saying that there is no honor among thieves, an idea that Falstaff touches on when he says, "A plague upon't when thieves cannot be true one to another!" (II.ii.25–26). Ironically, it is Harry—the crown prince himself—who is among the worst of the crew, not only participating in a robbery but also stabbing his friends in the back. This betrayal is done as a joke, but it is strangely at odds with Harry's alleged goal of becoming the most honorable character of all, one worthy of being a king. The questions raised here eventually culminate in the full-scale assault that Shakespeare (in the voice of Falstaff) launches, in Act V, scene i, on the ideal of honor, which Harry and the other noblemen claim to follow.

ACT II, SCENE IV

SUMMARY

At his family home (Warkworth Castle, in the far north of England), Hotspur reads a letter that has just arrived from a nobleman. Hotspur has asked the nobleman for support in the rebellion that the Percy family is planning against Henry. But the letter relays a refusal, saying that the Percy plot is not planned out well enough and that its allies are not strong or reliable enough to face so great a foe as Henry. Hotspur becomes very angry at the letter writer and disdains the writer's cowardice. He is concerned, however, that the writer will decide to reveal the plot to Henry, so he decides that he must set out that night to join his allies and start the rebellion.

Hotspur's wife, Lady Percy (also called Kate), comes in to speak to her husband. When Hotspur tells her that he will be leaving the castle within two hours, she becomes upset. She points out that for the past two weeks Hotspur has not eaten properly, slept well, or made love to her. Furthermore, he keeps on breaking out into a sweat in the middle of the night and crying out, babbling in his sleep about guns, cannons, prisoners, and soldiers. Lady Percy thinks that it is time Hotspur explained exactly what he's been planning.

Hotspur, however, ignores Lady Percy, instead instructing his servant to get his horse ready. Enraged, Lady Percy stops pleading and starts demanding answers. She suspects that Hotspur's machinations all have something to do with her brother, Lord Mortimer, and his claim to the throne. She threatens to break Hotspur's "little finger" (a euphemism for his penis) if he does not tell her what is going on (II.iv.79).

Hotspur abruptly turns on Lady Percy and angrily insults her, saying that he does not love her and that this is no world for womanly thoughts or for love. Instead, he declares, there must be war and fighting. He will not tell her what he is doing because he believes that women cannot be trusted, and she won't be able to reveal what she does not know. He concedes only that he will send for her, and that she may follow him on horseback the next day. Though dissatisfied, Lady Percy cannot get any more information from her belligerent husband.

ANALYSIS

Although this scene seems short and incidental, it is a telling portrait of gender and domestic life in the Renaissance. Hotspur's obsession with strategy and war make him a bad husband; he appears to think of his wife only as a sideline to his life as a fighter. Lady Percy reveals the emotional deficiency of the valiant Hotspur and provides a glimpse of the marital relations of the Elizabethan era. Neither husband nor wife is shy of alluding to sex, or a lack thereof. Renaissance women were considered to have a right to sexual pleasure from their husbands. Lady Percy has her sexual needs in mind when she complains that Hotspur has "given my treasures and my rights of thee / To thick-eyed musing and curst melancholy" (II.iv.39–40).

Despite this apparent liberation, Renaissance ideas of gender fell far short of promoting equal opportunity for men and women. Hotspur's refusal to confide in his wife is not unusual, nor is his belief that women cannot keep a secret. His words to Lady Percy— "constant you are, / But yet a woman"—demonstrate how he allows the stereotype that women are gossipmongers to outweigh his knowledge that Lady Percy herself is of a "constant" nature (II.iv.99–100). Hotspur's extreme machismo often endows him with a disturbingly violent perspective on the world, as when he bursts out: "This is no world / To play with maumets [dolls] and to tilt with lips [to kiss]. / We must have bloody noses and cracked crowns" (II.iv.82–84). In his thirst for war, Hotspur does not even admit love into his worldview; he is a knight without chivalry.

For her part, Lady Percy has few options: she can only accept whatever confidence her husband chooses to give her. For instance, when Hotspur asks whether his plan to let her follow him the next day will content her, she answers bitterly, "It must, of force" (II.iv.109). Here and throughout the Shakespearean tetralogy that deals with the English House of Lancaster, women generally have very little power. Both the dynamics of emotional attachment and the reshufflings of power occur solely among the male characters.

Though Hotspur's marriage is not really important to the overall plot of the play, Shakespeare still moves the plot forward considerably during this look into domestic life. By opening the scene with Hotspur reading the letter and concluding it with Hotspur preparing to leave for the rebellion, Shakespeare takes the civil war from its planning phase to the verge of actuality. Furthermore, by intertwining Lady Percy's complaints with observations about Hotspur's sleeplessness and preoccupation with war, we see not only Hotspur's treatment of his wife but also the extent of his obsession with the rebellion. Thus, in an extremely short scene, Shakespeare offers us a much deeper insight into Hotspur's character and also conveys the sense that the rebellion has undergone extensive planning and preparation. In this way, Shakespeare keeps the action moving forward without sacrificing the developing character studies at the heart of the play.

ACT II, SCENE V

SUMMARY

> *If sack and sugar be a fault, God help the wicked.*
> (See QUOTATIONS, p. 60)

In the Boar's Head Tavern in Eastcheap, London, Prince Harry is coming up out of the wine cellar. He has been drinking and making friends with the bartenders. He is clearly pleased that he has learned their names and their slang, like "dyeing scarlet," for example, which refers to chugging a mug of wine (II.v.13). Harry announces that these men, who like him, have called him "the king of courtesy, and . . . a good boy" (II.v.8–13). Harry meets Poins upstairs, and together they tease a young apprentice bartender named Francis.

Falstaff and his friends arrive, and Falstaff launches into the tale of how he and his friends were robbed just after they had committed their own robbery early that morning. As Falstaff tells Harry and Poins the story, his lies become more and more outrageous. For example, he claims that a hundred men set upon him and that he himself fought a dozen.

Finally, Harry cannot stand it anymore and confronts Falstaff with the truth. He and Poins know that only two robbers attacked Falstaff and the others because those robbers were Harry and Poins themselves in disguise. Falstaff, with his usual quick-wittedness, promptly bluffs his way out and says that he recognized Harry immediately when he and Poins attacked the party and that he only ran away to avoid having to hurt Harry. But he is glad to hear that Harry and Poins have the money, since now they can pay for everyone to get drunk.

The tavern's hostess, Mistress Quickly, comes in to tell Harry that his father has sent a nobleman to bring him a message. Falstaff goes to the door to get rid of the nobleman and returns with heavy news: civil war is brewing in England, and Harry must go to the court to see his father in the morning. The rebellious Percys and their many allies have all joined together to attack King Henry, and the king's beard has "turned white" with worry (II.v.328).

Harry and Falstaff decide to engage in a role-playing game so that Harry can prepare for his interview with his father the following morning. Falstaff will pretend to be King Henry and scold Harry, who then can practice his answers. In the role of the king, Falstaff bombastically defends himself to Harry, suggesting that even if Harry drops all his other rascally companions, he should keep the virtuous old Falstaff around. Harry, objecting that his father would not speak in this manner, suggests that he and Falstaff switch places. Now playing the role of King Henry, Harry rebukes Falstaff, who now plays the role of Harry, for hanging around with such a disreputable old man. Falstaff tries to defend himself, but he has trouble against Harry's sharp intelligence and regal bearing.

Harry and Falstaff's role-playing is interrupted when the sheriff and his night watch arrive at the tavern: they are looking for Falstaff and the others, who, they have learned, robbed the travelers on the highway early this morning. Harry tells Falstaff to hide and misdirects the sheriff by swearing to him that Falstaff is not there and that he himself will be responsible for finding the thief and turning him over. As the sheriff leaves, Harry finds Falstaff asleep where he was hiding. After picking Falstaff's pockets out of curiosity, Harry tells Peto that he will see his father in the morning and that all of them must go off to war. He adds that he will secure places in the army for all of his companions and place Falstaff in charge of a brigade of foot soldiers—a pointed joke, since Falstaff can hardly walk without running out of breath.

ANALYSIS

Harry's interlude with the bartenders, which occurs offstage, humorously illustrates his project of self-education, as he appears at the beginning of the scene after drinking with the young tavern men in the cellar. Harry evidently believes that establishing a connection with the common people—in this case by getting drunk with bartenders and by speaking their slang—is part of a useful education for kingship, an idea that his father does not share. The men's comment (as reported by Harry) that Harry is "but Prince of Wales yet … the king of courtesy" reflects how Harry's royal birth does not preclude the commoners from taking him as their fellow (II.v.9).

Falstaff's hilarious cascade of lies in recounting his encounter with the thieves who assaulted him is characteristic of his blustery, self-aggrandizing style. He clearly does not expect to be believed, since he changes his mind about the number of attackers at every other line; rather, he wants to entertain himself and his listeners. There are few better examples of Falstaff's resourcefulness and wittiness than his reaction to Harry's revelation that Harry and Poins were the only attackers. Without having to think about it for a moment, Falstaff responds with the brilliant response about not wanting to have to injure Harry that puts him in the right for having fled. His assertion that he recognized the pair allows him to praise himself along with Harry and to change the subject by ordering more wine.

The role-playing in which Falstaff and Harry engage at the end of the scene is both a spectacular display of wit and a complicated statement about the way the two think about each other and themselves. The style of Falstaff's speech to Harry, as he plays the role of

King Henry, derives from the over-the-top tragedies of Shakespeare's day; when Falstaff speaks "in King Cambyses' vein," he mocks the bombastic style of monarchs in such plays (II.v.352). Unsurprisingly, Falstaff praises the virtues of the "goodly, portly man" with whom Harry keeps company—Falstaff himself (II.v.384). When Harry takes over as King Henry, however, his mode of addressing Falstaff (now Harry) is harsher. The joke turns somewhat ugly; when he insults Falstaff, he does it thoroughly and painfully, labeling him "[t]hat villainous, abominable misleader of youth, . . . that old white-bearded Satan" (II.v.421–422).

There is a charged, foreboding sincerity in Falstaff's final plea to Harry in the role of the king. He begs Harry to banish the other ruffians "but for sweet Jack Falstaff, kind Jack Falstaff, true Jack Falstaff, valiant Jack Falstaff . . . Banish not him thy Harry's company, / Banish not him thy Harry's company" (II.v.432–437). Falstaff's description of himself as "sweet," "kind," "true," and "valiant" rings hollow, since Falstaff is quite clearly a cowardly robber who loves to exaggerate. But the repetition of his entreaty that Harry not banish him seems to endow his plea with a degree of seriousness and even melancholy, as if he senses that he ultimately will be banished. Indeed, Harry's brief, strange reply—"I do; I will"—has ominous overtones (II.v.439). This answer comes back to haunt Falstaff at the end of *1 Henry IV*'s sequel, *2 Henry IV*, when Harry does what seems unthinkable now: he does actually banish his dearest friend, along with the rest of the Eastcheap crowd.

Yet, in the conclusion of this tavern scene, Harry demonstrates an apparently spontaneous affection and goodwill toward Falstaff in lying outright to protect him from the sheriff. Falstaff, with typical casual ingratitude, has fallen asleep where he concealed himself. Harry's response of emptying out Falstaff's pockets—which contain nothing of value—seems a fair play among tavern regulars.

ACT III, SCENE I

SUMMARY
In Wales, at the castle of Owain Glyndŵr, the leaders of the rebel armies have gathered to discuss strategy. The two most important members of the Percy family, Hotspur and Worcester, are there, along with Lord Mortimer (Hotspur's brother-in-law, referred to in the play as his cousin). Their host, Glyndŵr, is Mortimer's father-in-

law and the leader of the Welsh rebels. He believes strongly in the ancient Welsh pagan traditions of prophecies, omens, magic, and demons. He claims to be able to call spirits from hell, and he says that at his birth the earth shook and the sky was full of fire. Hotspur makes fun of the Welsh leader's claims of magical power. Despite his best efforts, Mortimer cannot get his tactless brother-in-law to shut up. Hotspur mocks Glyndŵr's claim to be able to command the devil; Glyndŵr then asserts that he has repelled Henry's invasions three times. By the time the four actually get down to discussing strategy, Glyndŵr is none too pleased with his youngest guest.

The men take out a large map of Britain and divide it up as they have earlier discussed: after they defeat King Henry, Glyndŵr will get the western part of Britain—western England and all of Wales; Mortimer will get the southeast part of England, including London; Hotspur will get the northern part, home to his family. Hotspur begins to complain because he does not like the way that a river curves through his land, and he says that he will have the river straightened out. Irritated, Glyndŵr tells Hotspur that he must not do so, and the two bicker again, although Glyndŵr ends the dispute this time by giving in.

After Glyndŵr leaves the room, Mortimer chides Hotspur for bothering Glyndŵr. Hotspur says he is bored and annoyed with Glyndŵr's talk of prophecies and magic. Mortimer reminds him that Glyndŵr is a powerful, courageous, and well-read man, and also possibly a dangerous magician. He points out that Glyndŵr has been very tolerant of Hotspur's youthful obnoxiousness. Anyone else, he warns, would have felt the force of Glyndŵr's anger already. Worcester agrees and urges Hotspur to mind his manners and show respect. Hotspur claims unconvincingly that he has learned his lesson.

Glyndŵr brings in Mortimer's and Hotspur's wives; the four must say goodbye, for the men must ride off to meet their allies that very night. Lady Mortimer, Glyndŵr's daughter, cannot speak English, and Mortimer knows no Welsh. Lady Mortimer weeps for her husband, who speaks lovingly to her, and Glyndŵr translates between them. Mortimer lays his head in her lap, and she sings the company a song in Welsh. Meanwhile, Hotspur and his wife, Lady Percy, bid each other farewell in a half-affectionate, half-fighting manner. By the time Lady Mortimer's song is over, the formal contracts of agreement among the rebel leaders have been drawn up. The men sign them, and Mortimer, Hotspur, and Worcester then set forth. They are heading to Shrewsbury, near the English border with Wales, to meet the Earl of Northumberland (Hotspur's father) and his ally, the Douglas of Scotland, who will bring with him a thousand soldiers. Glyndŵr, meanwhile, will gather his army, which he plans to lead into England within two weeks.

ANALYSIS

Hotspur's quick temper and insolence flare up once again in this scene: with a few rude words, he alienates the extremely powerful Owain Glyndŵr, one of his family's most important allies. By this point, Hotspur's immaturity is apparent as the negative side of his boldness and sharp military instincts. As Worcester insightfully notes, Hotspur's greatest asset—his boldness and quick temper—is also his worst flaw; he is valiant in battle but cannot manipulate or work with people behind the scenes. This flaw eventually proves a deadly weakness for Hotspur, since manipulation and diplomacy are among the greatest strengths of Prince Harry, his archrival. This tension emphasizes the importance the play places on understanding the qualities of true leadership.

This scene also provides us with a strong taste of Welsh culture and tradition, which Glyndŵr embodies. The English regarded the ancient Welsh customs and supernatural traditions with mingled disdain and unease. On the one hand, they felt that a more advanced civilization (as they considered themselves) should have no fear of ancient superstitions. On the other hand, however, no one could be sure that the Welsh were not really magicians. This scene recalls the horror with which Westmoreland speaks, in Act I, scene i, about the ritualistic mutilations that the Welsh women performed upon the English dead.

Glyndŵr himself is a fascinating mix of the Welsh and English worlds. As he rather sternly reminds the insolent Hotspur, he was "trained up in the English court" and speaks fluent English as well as his native Welsh (III.i.119); as Mortimer further notes, he is "exceedingly well read"—a quality associated with gentlemanliness and urban sophistication (III.i.162). But Glyndŵr's claims to be a magician able to summon demons, along with his insistence on the significance of the omens that he believes filled the sky and earth on the day of his birth, reflects his strong commitment to his pagan heritage. Even Mortimer implies that he believes in Glyndŵr's magic arts, testifying that Glyndŵr is "profited / In strange concealments," or supernatural skills (III.i.162–163).

SUMMARY & ANALYSIS

Hotspur rudely trivializes Glyndŵr's claims to magic and justified patriotism. To Glyndŵr's boasts about defeating Henry's attempted invasions and sending him home "[b]ootless," Hotspur exclaims in mock surprise, "Home without boots, and in foul weather too!" (III.i.64–65). Given the gravity of the situation, Hotspur's punning response at Glyndŵr's expense is inappropriate.

Mortimer's inability to communicate with his own wife is a further manifestation of the cultural barriers between the English and the Welsh. Unlike Hotspur, however, Mortimer at least shows himself to be aware of the value of understanding other cultures and tongues, despairing, "O, I am ignorance itself in this!" when he cannot understand his wife (III.i.206). The presumably exotic song that Shakespeare has Lady Mortimer sing in Welsh would probably have established a sense of the foreign and the mysterious for an Elizabethan audience—a taste of the "irregular and wild" world that lay just beyond the bounds of late medieval and Renaissance English civilization (I.i.40).

Act III, scene ii

Summary

Prince Harry has come to the royal palace, after a long absence, to answer his father's summons. Henry is both sad and angry and rebukes his son in stinging terms. He says he would like to be able to forgive Harry but he cannot tolerate Harry's recent behavior. Henry asserts that if Harry continues to hang around with commoners, he will never command the respect a king must have. Henry feels that familiarity breeds contempt: only that which is rare and unusual is well respected. When he himself was waging the war that made him a king, he adds, he didn't slum around London the way Harry does. Rather, when he made his occasional appearances, he was very courteous and regal. That way, the common people respected and loved him in a way that they do not respect or love Harry.

Henry then tells Harry that he is behaving just like Richard II (the king whom Henry overthrew): the common people scorned and hated Richard, who spent too much time indulging in pleasures and who made friends and counselors out of fools. In Henry's opinion, such dissolute behavior will make the people hate Harry too.

Henry continues his diatribe against Harry, saying that he feels that Hotspur currently has more real right than Harry to inherit the throne. For, although Harry has the claim of blood inheritance, Hotspur is the one who demonstrates his courage in warfare, winning honor in his battles and daring to take on even the king himself. While Hotspur reminds Henry of himself when he was young, Henry does not recognize himself at all in Harry. In fact, it is clear (according to Henry) that Harry acts like such a scoundrel because he hates his father. Henry is sure that Harry will soon go over to Hotspur's side, joining forces with Henry's deadly enemies.

Clearly moved, Harry breaks out into an emotional speech in which he asserts that Henry is wrong. He swears that he will take revenge upon Hotspur for everything that Hotspur has ever done against Henry. He adds that when he finally defeats Hotspur in combat, all of Hotspur's honor, glories, and achievements will become Harry's own. He vows to begin acting in a way suitable to the heir to the throne, and he solemnly declares that he will carry out what he has sworn or die in the attempt. Pleased but wary, Henry tells Harry that he may have the command of soldiers in the upcoming war, to prove himself sincere and carry out his vow.

Sir Walter Blunt, one of Henry's trusted allies, enters suddenly, bearing the news that the Douglas, the leader of the Scottish rebels, met the English rebels several days earlier at Shrewsbury, in the west of England. The combined force will soon be ready to attack. Henry says that he already knows about this development and has sent out his younger son, Prince John (Lord of Lancaster), and the Earl of Westmoreland to meet them. Next Wednesday, he adds, Harry will set out, and on Thursday, Henry and his forces will follow. All will meet at Bridgnorth, not far from the rebels' camp at Shrewsbury, in twelve days.

ANALYSIS

This critical scene is positioned at the midpoint of the play, halfway through the third act. Shakespeare often places the important turning point of a play at the midpoint, neatly dividing the action into prelude and result. The most obvious importance of this scene is that Harry vows to abandon his vagabond ways and behave as a royal prince should. He has long planned to undergo this transformation, as he earlier reveals (he plans to redeem himself "when men think least I will" [I.ii.195]). Evidently, with his father despairing and war looming nearer, Harry decides that the time is right to make his move.

The crucial moment, when it comes, is surprisingly brief and understated. In the midst of his father's long speech of reproof, Harry gives a reply of a single sentence, saying simply, "I shall hereafter, my thrice-gracious lord, / Be more myself" (III.ii.92–93). Harry's words imply that the seedy, lazy image he has projected to the public is not his *real* self and that he has only been playing an elaborate game. Now, it appears, he feels it is time to throw off the pretense and reveal his true, kingly nature.

Harry follows this brief but heartfelt promise with a much longer and more elaborate speech after his father has finished speaking. Here, he makes clear the terms of his commitment to reform and vows to do specific things to prove it: he acknowledges his past faults, begs his father's forgiveness, swears never to return to those ways again, and promises to prove himself by fighting and defeating Hotspur. Harry finally makes concrete the connection between himself and Hotspur that Shakespeare has hinted at all along—that Hotspur is winning the glory that rightly should belong to Harry. Harry's belief that Hotspur is merely his "factor," or stand-in, and that Hotspur's defeat will prove Harry's nobility contributes to the sense that a final confrontation between the two young Harrys is inevitable (III.ii.147).

The confrontation between the royal father and son in Act III, scene ii echoes several earlier moments. Shakespeare is fond of symmetries and often repeats scenes, conversations, or even characters. Harry and Hotspur form a symmetrical pair, as do Falstaff and Henry—both are father figures to Harry, but Harry can accept them only alternatingly, one at a time. The scene itself mirrors the role-playing game that Harry and Falstaff stage in the latter half of Act II, scene iv. But it also echoes Harry's own vow to himself at the end of Act I, scene ii, especially in terms of its use of language and metaphor. Most noticeable is the use of the sun as a symbol of the king and his reign. While Henry alludes to the lack of "sun-like majesty" of the previous king, Richard II (III.ii.79), Harry earlier states that he will "imitate the sun, / . . . / By breaking through the foul and ugly mists" (I.ii.175–180). Since Harry has now cast off his pretense of idleness, he will presumably soon burn through the clouds and begin to shine with the sun's terrifying radiance.

ACT III, SCENE III

SUMMARY

In the Boar's Head Tavern in London, Falstaff complains to Bardolph about how thin and weak he has gotten of late (an obviously ridiculous claim for the hugely fat Falstaff to make). The hostess of the tavern, Mistress Quickly, appears and demands payment from Falstaff for the food and drink he has consumed, as well as for some clothing she has recently bought for him. Falstaff responds that his pocket was picked the previous night while he was asleep, and he accuses her of having done it. He claims to have had money and a valuable ring in the pocket. The hostess accuses Falstaff of trying to get out of paying his bill, but their argument is interrupted by the entrance of Prince Harry and Peto.

Harry's news is unsurprising but important: war is at hand, and all must go off to fight. But first, the group must settle the matter of Falstaff's picked pocket. After some bawdy teasing at the expense of the dim-witted hostess, Harry reveals that he himself emptied Falstaff's pockets the night before (as detailed in Act II, scene v) and that he found nothing in them but tavern bills, receipts from whorehouses, and a handful of candy. Falstaff, with his usual quickwittedness, promptly weasels out of admitting wrongdoing once again, tells the hostess that he forgives her, and orders breakfast.

Harry informs Falstaff that he has bailed him out yet again: he has paid back the money that Falstaff and the others had stolen and lost the day before. Finally, he gets around to assigning the war commissions to his friends. He sends Bardolph off to deliver letters on horseback to King Henry's troops, who are already on their way—one letter to Harry's younger brother, John, Lord of Lancaster, another to the Earl of Westmoreland. He orders Peto to come on a different errand with him, and he tells Falstaff that he has put him in charge of a brigade of foot soldiers, commanding him to meet him the following afternoon to get the details of the commission. All business now, Harry departs on his military errand with Peto. Falstaff, for his part, does not plan to let the war effort come between him and a good breakfast.

ANALYSIS

This little scene is largely an exercise in wit, full of Falstaff's easy bantering with Bardolph, the hostess Mistress Quickly, and Harry. Like so many of Falstaff's other scenes, this one entertains and adds a depth and humor to the play (especially in performance), but unlike some of the play's other seemingly incidental scenes, this one carries little in the way of plot development. On some level, Falstaff's jokes must simply be enjoyed rather than analyzed in depth.

We do see an excellent example here of Falstaff's ability to adapt swiftly to change. His reaction to being trapped in a lie is the same as in the earlier scene of the foiled highway robbery: he pretends he was managing the situation all along and turns it to his advantage. In this case, he turns the fact that he was pickpocketed into an accusation of the hostess, enabling him to deflect her demands for payment. Falstaff exaggerates the cheap "eightpenny matter" of his lost ring (III.iii.94) into a valuable object worth the large sum of "forty mark" (III.iii.73), and he pretends that the shirts the hostess bought him were made of coarse material. He lets no opportunity for his own betterment slip by, even at the cost of telling quite extraordinary lies. When Harry catches him barefaced in his falsehood about the lost money, Falstaff weasels out with marvelous adroitness and lands on his feet by making himself the victim of Harry's thievery. He is so successful in turning the situation on its head that he even *forgives* the hostess and compels her to fetch him breakfast.

This scene also spotlights the continuing ambivalence in the relationship between Harry and Falstaff. Their verbal sparring here seems to be largely affectionate, and Harry has done Falstaff another unsolicited kindness: after hiding him from the sheriff the night before, he has paid back in full the money that Falstaff's party stole on the highway. While Harry considers himself a "good angel" to Falstaff for returning the money, it seems possible that the desire to protect himself from any serious criminal charges is also one of Harry's motivations, since he is, after all, partially responsible for the theft (III.iii.163). Furthermore, while Harry has procured Falstaff a good position—a command of infantry soldiers—in the upcoming war, in doing so he has rehashed the Act II, scene ii joke about Falstaff's distaste for walking.

Despite the comedy attached to the notion of Falstaff on foot again, Harry has begun to take the war very seriously. His remark that "[t]he land is burning, Percy stands on high, / And either we or they must lower lie" reveals his understanding of the gravity of the situation—he is well aware that one side and one side only will prevail in this high-stakes battle (III.iii.187–188). Falstaff acts as a foil for Harry: whereas Harry respects his opponent, Falstaff issues a cynical declaration of praise about the Percy clan ("Well, God be thanked for these rebels—they offend none but the virtuous" [III.iii.174–175]). Additionally, whereas Harry focuses on the upcoming battle, Falstaff thinks of nothing but gratifying his physical desire for food, shouting, "Hostess, my breakfast come!— / O, I could wish this tavern were my drum!" (III.iii.189–190). His silly closing rhyme of "come!" and "drum!" parodies Harry's solemn closing rhyme of "high" and "lie."

ACT IV, SCENES I–II

SUMMARY: ACT IV, SCENE I

In the rebels' base camp in Shrewsbury (in the west of England, near the Welsh border), Hotspur, Worcester, and the Douglas are discussing their strategy of attack when a messenger arrives bearing bad news. Hotspur's father, Northumberland, is very sick and has decided not to lead his troops to Hotspur—or to send them at all. Worcester is deeply disturbed by this news, since not only will Northumberland's absence seriously weaken the rebel forces, but it will also betray to the world that the rebels are divided among themselves. Hotspur, however, quickly manages to convince himself that all is well and bounces back optimistically.

Another messenger arrives, Sir Richard Vernon, who is a relative of the Percys. Vernon has information that Henry's forces, commanded by the Earl of Westmoreland and Henry's younger son, Prince John, are marching toward Shrewsbury with seven thousand men. Moreover, the king himself and the Prince of Wales—Harry—are also approaching with still more forces. Vernon has seen Harry bearing himself regally in his armor: he strikes all who see him as an excellent horseman and an awe-inspiring young soldier. Unintimidated, Hotspur expresses a wish to meet Harry in single combat to the death.

But Vernon has still more bad news: Glyndŵr has sent word from Wales that he will not be able to assemble his forces within the allotted fourteen days. This development is very alarming to both Worcester and the Douglas, since the battle will clearly occur before Glyndŵr can arrive. Hotspur, however, refuses to let anything sway his confidence: even if they must die, they will die merrily. The Douglas, recovering from the alarming news, claims to have no fear of death at all, and the men continue to plan their battle.

SUMMARY: ACT IV, SCENE II

Meanwhile, on the road near Coventry—in southeastern England, east of London—Falstaff and his men are marching west toward their rendezvous with Henry at Bridgnorth. Falstaff sends Bardolph to buy some wine, and, while Bardolph is gone, Falstaff talks aloud about his methods for finding his unit of foot soldiers. Falstaff proves a very corrupt military captain, which is not surprising. Instead of using his power of impressment (that is, the power to draft soldiers) to draft the best fighters available into his division, he has instead targeted wealthy merchants and farmers who want to stay home. These individuals are willing to bribe Falstaff in order to get out of the service. As a result, Falstaff has made a good deal of money for himself, but his troops consist only of ragtag souls willing to let themselves be hired as soldiers: kleptomaniac house servants, youngest sons with no inheritance, and bankrupt laborers. They are mostly undernourished, untrustworthy, and unimpressive.

While Falstaff waits for Bardolph to return, Harry and Henry's ally, the Earl of Westmoreland, comes down the road and take him by surprise. Westmoreland casts a dubious eye upon Falstaff's conscripts, but Falstaff cheerfully tells him that they are good enough for cannon fodder. Harry warns Falstaff that he must hurry, for Hotspur and the Percy allies are already preparing to fight, and Henry has already made camp at Bridgnorth. The group hurries westward to meet Henry.

ANALYSIS: ACT IV, SCENES I–II

Just as the play builds in drama to Harry's vow to redeem himself in Act III, scene ii, it now builds toward resolution: the Battle of Shrewsbury (which occurs in Act V). The course that the play must take from here, however, is already becoming clear: the cascade of bad news that pours in on the Percys in Act IV, scene i seems to indicate the beginning of the end. Abandoned by their allies one by one, the rebels—already the underdogs against the entrenched power and divine right of King Henry—are seeing their chances for victory worsen by the minute.

We get a sense of the Percys' poor prospects for victory from Worcester's reaction to the developments. Throughout the play, he has shown himself to be the mastermind behind the Percys' schemes and to be a sounder judge of character and policy than his impulsive nephew. Against Worcester's pragmatic assessment of the situation, Hotspur's rather maniacal and desperate insistence on optimism begins to look unrealistic. Hotspur even begins to sound a bit absurd, as, in response to the news that his father will not be bringing his troops, he declares that Northumberland's absence is "[a] perilous gash, a very limb lopped off. / And yet, in faith, it is not" (IV.i.43–44). With characteristic rashness, he leaps to a conclusion without thinking it through or justifying it. Furthermore, he proves as resolved in his decisions to act as in his opinions. Intoxicated by the prospect of approaching war and in fierce denial about the weakened chances of his side, Hotspur departs with a sort of mad cheerfulness, declaring, "Come, let us take a muster speedily. / Doomsday is near: die all, die merrily" (IV.i.134–135).

While the laconic Douglas, who seems to pride himself on his fearlessness and his few words, agrees with Hotspur's baseless self-confidence, Worcester is more thoughtful and, thus, more concerned about the situation. He realizes that other leaders upon whose help the Percys depend may believe that Northumberland is staying away out of fear and lack of trust. It would be disastrous, Worcester notes, if fear on the part of other rebel forces were to "breed a kind of question in our cause" (IV.i.68). Worcester realizes that if the rebels fail to present a united front, they may find their supporters slipping away in a disastrous chain reaction. Indeed, with Vernon's announcement that Glyndŵr will not be able to bring his troops until it is too late, the chain reaction seems to have begun. Whether Glyndŵr has decided to hold back because he has heard of Northumberland's decision or because of some superstition, it is clear that the fortunes of war are turning against the Percys.

This scene also continues the symbolic establishment of Harry and Hotspur as opposites. Through Vernon's report, Shakespeare presents the newly reformed Prince Harry, making good on his promises to his father. Vernon's famous description of Harry shows us a deft, handsome, and thoroughly impressive young warrior-prince, "[a]s full of spirit as the month of May, / And gorgeous as the sun at midsummer; / Wanton as youthful goats, wild as young bulls" (IV.i.102–104). When Vernon compares Harry to "feathered Mercury" (the Roman messenger god, who wore winged sandals and a winged hat) and an "angel" riding Pegasus (the famous winged horse of Greek mythology), Hotspur cuts him off abruptly, unable to stomach hearing about his illustrious rival (IV.i.107–110).

With this language, Shakespeare makes it clear that Harry has at last come to challenge Hotspur for his glory: the images of divine warriors and particularly the emphasis on "noble horsemanship" have been attributed to Hotspur in the past (IV.i.111). (Hotspur's nickname itself suggests a fiery-tempered, impatient horseman.) Like Harry, Hotspur knows now that he must challenge Harry, since only one of them can claim the honor that they both want. His statement that "Harry to Harry shall, hot horse to horse, / Meet and ne'er part till one drop down a corpse" (IV.i.123–124) echoes Harry's earlier declaration that "[t]he land is burning, Percy stands on high, / And either we or they must lower lie" (III.iii.187–188).

ACT IV, SCENES III–IV

SUMMARY: ACT IV, SCENE III
At the rebels' camp in Shrewsbury, Hotspur and the Douglas argue with Worcester about whether they ought to attack Henry's forces right away or hold off for a while. Worcester and Vernon urge them to wait: not all of the forces that Vernon will send have arrived yet, and since Worcester's band of knights on horses has just arrived that day, the horses are still worn out. But Hotspur and the Douglas are both impatient to attack.

Sir Walter Blunt arrives in their camp, bearing an offer of peace from Henry. If Hotspur and his allies will state their grievances against Henry and disband their attack, he says, Henry promises that he will satisfy their desires and grant full amnesty to the rebels. Hotspur then launches into a long speech in which he describes his family's dissatisfaction with Henry: when Henry himself had been the underdog several years before, trying to seize power from the king at the time, Richard II, the Percy family gave him invaluable help. Henry, then known as Henry Bolingbroke, had once been a mere cousin of the former king. Exiled by his royal cousin for flimsy reasons, Henry returned to England while King Richard was away fighting in Ireland. He originally claimed that he had only come to reclaim the title and inheritance that were due to him from his father, Richard's recently deceased uncle, whose lands Richard had seized upon his death. Henry stayed, of course, to fight for the crown of England. Partly swayed by the influence and power of the Percy family, the common people of England and the nobles of Richard's court joined Henry's faction, allowing him to take over power from Richard in a bloodless coup—though Richard was later assassinated in mysterious circumstances.

Now, King Henry seems to have forgotten the gratitude he owes the Percy family—the most recent example being his refusal to pay a ransom for Mortimer after Mortimer was captured in Wales. Blunt asks if he should take Hotspur's words as a declaration of war; Hotspur replies that Blunt should return to Henry and await Worcester in the morning with the rebels' decision. Hotspur suggests they may decide to accept Henry's offer of amnesty after all.

Summary: Act IV, scene iv

Meanwhile, in York (in northern England), the Archbishop of York, an ally of Hotspur and the other rebels, speaks with a friend named Sir Michael. The archbishop gives Sir Michael urgent letters, including one to the archbishop's cousin Scrope and another to the Lord Marshal. He tells Sir Michael anxiously that the next day will be very important, stating that the "fortune of ten thousand men" depends on the outcome of the battle that is to occur at Shrewsbury (IV.iv.9). He is very concerned, for he has heard that Henry's forces are powerful and that with Northumberland, Glyndŵr, and Mortimer absent, the Percy forces will be too weak to emerge victorious.

Sir Michael bids the archbishop be optimistic, since the rebellion does have on its side powerful warriors like the Douglas, his son Mordake, Vernon, Hotspur, Worcester, and others. But the archbishop replies that the king has all the other finest warriors in the land, including the Prince of Wales (Harry), his younger brother, Prince John, Westmoreland, Blunt, and many more. The archbishop urges Sir Michael to make haste with the letters. Apparently, the archbishop plans to set up a contingency plan in case Henry wins at Shrewsbury. He knows that Henry is aware of his involvement in the uprising, and, if the rebels lose, the archbishop will be implicated in the conspiracy.

Analysis: Act IV, scenes iii–iv

The heart of Act IV, scene iii is Hotspur's recounting of the history behind the Percys' grievances against King Henry. Shakespeare's audience would have been familiar with the events that Hotspur describes, since they were then a matter of relatively recent history. Moreover, other plays of the era had related these events, including Shakespeare's own *Richard II*, which appeared about a year or so prior to *1 Henry IV*.

Hotspur's accusations in this scene are somewhat hypocritical, since he seems to imply that his father, Northumberland, only helped Henry to power because he believed that Henry would not overthrow the rightful king ("he heard him swear and vow to God / He came but to be Duke of Lancaster" [IV.iii.62–63]). The reality is, of course, somewhat more complicated, however, and it seems that Northumberland and the other Percys must have known perfectly well from the outset that Henry wanted to become king. Their choice to throw their power behind Henry in a claim to lands being held by King Richard could owe only to their confidence that Henry would overtake Richard, for if Henry were to fail, they would face serious retribution from King Richard. The complexity of the characters' mixed political motivations seems to cast doubt on Hotspur's own claim that he and his family have gathered their current army only in order to preserve their own safety.

Hotspur's statement that the rebels may decide to accept Henry's offer of peace is rather unexpected given Hotspur's generally warlike character. It is completely at odds with his vow in the preceding section to fight Harry to the death. It is also an important point to bear in mind when Shakespeare reveals, in Act V, that Worcester is keeping certain facts from Hotspur because he fears that his nephew will be inclined to settle the debate peacefully. Worcester, not wanting a peaceful solution, thus secretly squelches any opportunity for Hotspur to follow through on the rational impulse that he shows in this scene.

The Archbishop of York's only appearance in *1 Henry IV* occurs in this scene, whose purpose is to set up plot threads that extend into the next play in Shakespeare's sequence—*2 Henry IV*. We do not learn much about what the archbishop's letters contain, but their effects imply that plots are being laid that will continue to haunt Henry even after the Battle of Shrewsbury concludes. Indeed, when the battle has scarcely ended, in Act V, scene v, Henry must almost immediately divide and disperse his forces again—half northward toward York and Northumberland, where the archbishop and the one remaining Percy are arming themselves, and half to Wales to deal with Glyndŵr and his rebels.

ACT V, SCENES I–II

SUMMARY: ACT V, SCENE I

[H]onour pricks me on . . . Therefore I'll none of it.
Honour is a mere scutcheon. (See QUOTATIONS, p. 61)

In their camp at Shrewsbury, Henry and Harry watch the sun rise, red and dim, on the morning of the all-important battle. Worcester and Vernon arrive as messengers from the rebel camp, and Henry addresses Worcester, asking if he is willing to avoid the conflict, which will inevitably be destructive, and make peace. Worcester says that he would have avoided the conflict if he could have but that Henry's behavior has made doing so impossible. He takes up Hotspur's accusations to Blunt in Act IV, scene iii, reminding Henry that the Percy family gave him assistance when Henry was still the underdog and that, without their help, Henry never could have overthrown Richard II. He says that Henry has become so forgetful of his debts and so hostile toward the Percys lately that the family feels that it has no choice but to flee from court and raise an army to bring about justice.

Henry dismisses these charges as mere excuses, declaring that those who are discontented for small and petty reasons and who are driven by the lust for power can always find some reason to try to overthrow those currently in power. Harry then offers a solution: he bids Worcester tell Hotspur that, since the whole world knows what a valiant knight Hotspur is, Harry himself will meet Hotspur in single combat to decide the conflict. This way, he proposes, the many men who would die in a full-fledged battle will be spared.

Worcester departs, and Harry and Henry agree that the rebels probably will not accept the offer—Hotspur and the Douglas are both too confident of their chances in pitched battle. Henry departs to prepare his troops, and Harry and Falstaff say their last goodbyes before the fight. After Harry leaves, Falstaff muses about the worthlessness of honor, suggesting that only dead men can keep it— although they get no benefit from it—while the living are forced to suffer on honor's behalf.

SUMMARY: ACT V, SCENE II

In the rebel camp in Shrewsbury, Worcester has decided not to tell Hotspur about Henry's respectful offer of amnesty or Harry's challenge to single combat. Worcester is afraid that Hotspur would accept the offer of peace, which he does not want: Worcester is sure that if a truce were made and the Percys returned to living under Henry's rule, he and Northumberland would never be left in peace. Even if Henry forgave Hotspur because of his youth, Worcester reasons, he and Northumberland would always be watched, and no matter what they did, they would eventually be accused of treachery. Worcester thus selfishly decides to keep the recent offers secret.

Worcester lies to Hotspur, telling him that Henry insulted the Percys and mocked their grievances. The rash Hotspur immediately sends off a challenge via a messenger, demanding that Henry meet the Percys on the battlefield. Only then does Worcester tell him about Harry's offer to meet him in single combat, and Hotspur declares that he will seek Harry out on the battlefield and engage him one on one. A messenger arrives with urgent letters for Hotspur, but Hotspur, impetuous as ever, decides that he does not have time to read them. He and the other leaders withdraw to prepare their troops for battle.

ANALYSIS: ACT V, SCENES I–II

The confrontation between Worcester and King Henry in Act V, scene i almost duplicates the one in Act IV, scene iii, in which Hotspur accuses Blunt in similar terms. Worcester's speech and Henry's reply help to remind us of the ambiguity that surrounds all the political motivations in the play: Worcester offers a formidable list of justifications for the Percys' rising against Henry, citing the king's "unkind usage, dangerous countenance, / And violation of all faith and troth" (V.i.69–70). In a rebuke loaded with disdainful sarcasm, Henry points out that "never yet did insurrection want / Such water-colours to impaint his cause"—that is, insurrections always find a way to color their cause as the righteous one (V.i.79–80). It remains ambiguous whether Henry is right, or if the Percys are justified in their complaints. As usual, Shakespeare refuses to offer us a simple answer.

In Act V, scene i, Harry appears onstage manifesting his kingly nature for the first time since his memorable vow of redemption in Act III, scene ii. In both acknowledging his former follies—"I may speak it to my shame, / I have a truant been to chivalry"—and in offering, in highly respectful terms, to meet Hotspur in single combat, Harry demonstrates that he has indeed matured into a man fit to lead (V.i.93–94). It is clear that the "noble deeds" and fine qualities that Harry praises in Hotspur are those that he himself aims to attain (V.i.92).

Falstaff's monologue on honor at the end of Act V, scene i offers key insight into his character. Falstaff seems to be trying to undermine the very standards that the noble contenders hold so dear: in this famous speech, he weighs the emptiness of the proud word "honor" against the losses its pursuit can bring. He says that "honour pricks me on," parroting the party line; but he then discredits it, complaining, "[y]ea, but how if honour prick me off [kills me] when I come on? How then?" (V.i.129–130). Honor, he muses, cannot replace or heal a lost or wounded limb. It is of no use to the living, and the dead cannot use it either. He concludes that "Honor is a mere scutcheon"—a heraldic device used at funerals, nothing more than a flimsy decoration for the coffins of the dead (V.i.138). Falstaff's worldly and philosophical logic throws a harsh light on the values that drive the nobility into a battle certain to leave thousands dead.

In Act V, scene ii, Worcester reveals himself to be quite a manipulator. His decision to conceal Harry's and Henry's offers from Hotspur in order to protect his own future welfare comes as a surprise. His reference to his nephew as "hare-brained Hotspur, govern'd by a spleen [a hot temper]" also reveals Worcester's awareness of Hotspur's dispositional and intellectual limitations (V.ii.19). He has read Hotspur perfectly, for Hotspur sends a challenge to Henry the moment he hears about the alleged slurs against his family. With his usual haste, Hotspur is taken in by Worcester's words and, fulfilling the king's prediction in Act V, scene i, commits his army to a bloody war for which it may not be ready.

ACT V, SCENES III–V

SUMMARY: ACT V, SCENE III

On the battlefield at Shrewsbury, the fight is on between the army of King Henry and the forces of the Percy rebellion. The Douglas, the fearless leader of the Scotsmen, searches the battlefield for Henry himself. He meets Sir Walter Blunt, dressed like the king and acting as a decoy. The two fight, and the Douglas kills Blunt. Hotspur enters and identifies the dead Blunt as an impostor.

The two leave in search of the real Henry, and Falstaff appears, trying to avoid the heat of the battle. He encounters a breathless Harry, who has lost his sword. Harry asks Falstaff if he can borrow his. The cowardly Falstaff declines to give it up—if Hotspur is still alive, Falstaff does not want to be unarmed. Disgusted, Harry leaves, and Falstaff goes off in a different direction.

SUMMARY: ACT V, SCENE IV

Harry reenters, now accompanied by his father, brother John, and Westmoreland. Harry is wounded but refuses to stop fighting and seek medical attention. He heads off with John and Westmoreland to fight, leaving Henry alone. The Douglas reenters, still seeking the king. Henry bravely meets the Douglas in single combat, although he knows that he can hardly hope to win: he is an old man, while the Douglas is a deadly fighter in the prime of his life. Harry reappears, and, seeing his father in danger, challenges the Douglas, whom he beats back so ferociously that the Douglas flees the field. Henry thanks his son with warmth and pride, saying he has at last regained his father's respect, and Harry heads back into battle.

Hotspur enters and finds Harry alone. They identify one another, and both agree that it is time they fought to the death. In the heat of their battle, Falstaff wanders back in. The fighters do not notice him, but Falstaff cheers Harry on. The Douglas returns once again and attacks Falstaff. Falstaff falls down, pretending to be dead, and the Douglas leaves him where he lies.

Harry, meanwhile, has critically wounded Hotspur, who dies. Spying Falstaff lying on the ground as if dead, Harry eulogizes both and, vowing to come back and bury them, leaves. As soon as Harry is gone, Falstaff springs up and stabs the dead Hotspur in the leg. When Harry and John reenter, Falstaff, in his typical manner, claims that he fought a bloody battle with the wounded Hotspur after Harry left and finally finished him off. John and the dumbfounded Harry decide to settle the matter later. They hear the trumpets sounding retreat, and all return together to the base camp.

SUMMARY: ACT V, SCENE V

The battle is over, and Henry's forces have won decisively. The rebel leaders are all dead or captured. Henry, who has discovered that the battle was triggered, in part, by Worcester's intentional failure to deliver his offer of peace to Hotspur, orders Worcester and Vernon to be executed.

News arrives that the Douglas has been captured. Harry, asking his father for permission to handle the case, commands that the Douglas be set free in recognition of his valor and integrity. Henry, realizing that there are still powerful rebels left alive, makes plans to deal with them: he will send John and Westmoreland to York to deal with Northumberland and the archbishop, who he knows are up in arms against him. Meanwhile, Prince Harry, he says, will come with him to Wales to deal with Mortimer and Owain Glyndŵr.

ANALYSIS: ACT V, SCENES III–V

These very short, very busy scenes, which show us the progress of the battle at Shrewsbury, represent the main climax toward which the earlier portions of the play have been building. Nearly all the factions have finally been brought together in a single compressed, action-packed battle—marked by frenetically paced entrances and exits and clashes in single combat.

Falstaff's battlefield interpretation of honor in this final section of the play provides both amusement and food for thought. When he stumbles across the body of Sir Walter Blunt (slain, ironically, because he is thought to be King Henry), his immediate comment is: "Sir Walter Blunt. There's honour for you. Here's no vanity" (V.iii.32–33). His jab about "vanity" is ironic. Falstaff seems to be commenting sarcastically on the extreme vanity, or folly, of Blunt's death—if "honor" is what has led to his lying cold on the ground, then "honor" seems utterly useless.

Falstaff's thoughtful linking of honor with death and his preference for life are vividly illustrated in the next scene, when Falstaff seems to die and then return to life. In some respect, Falstaff enacts a bizarre and playful mockery of war and death: in addition to carrying around a bottle of wine where his gun should be, he pretends to be killed honorably in battle, receives a eulogy from Harry, and then rises up, pretending that he has conquered a nobleman. Not even the danger of the field can stop him from punning. With his inimitable Falstaffian logic, he defends his own honor in these actions: "The better part of valour is discretion, in the which better part I have saved my life" (V.iv.117–118). Falstaff's views on honor, though they are unlike those of the noblemen fighting and dying on the battlefield, are oddly convincing—perhaps especially so because, unlike so many of the noblemen, Falstaff ends up alive.

Harry resolves two of his own important conflicts during this battle. First, he finally resolves the tension between himself and his father. When he rescues Henry from the attack of the Douglas, Henry's response is complex but wholly approving. Not only is he proud of his warlike son, but he also seems to have been genuinely concerned that his son did not care about him ("Thou hast redeemed thy lost opinion, / And showed thou mak'st some tender of my life" [V.iv.47–48]). Harry responds in equally heartfelt terms—"O God, they did me too much injury / That ever said I hearkened for your death"—that further distinguish him from Hotspur; for while Hotspur seeks to overthrow Henry, Harry seeks to preserve him (V.iv.50–51).

Second, Harry finally confronts Hotspur, and the two engage in their long-anticipated duel. Harry's commanding announcement when he faces Hotspur that "[t]wo stars keep not their motion in one sphere" shows his perception of them as rivals who cannot coexist (V.iv.64). While both men idealize valor, in the end, they seem to have somewhat different approaches to the question that Falstaff raises earlier about the relationship between honor and death. Even as he is dying, Hotspur mourns more for his glory than for his life: "I better brook the loss of brittle life / Than those proud titles thou hast won of me" (V.iv.77–78). But Harry, contemplating Hotspur's corpse, brings forth a famous contemplation on the humility enforced by death:

> When that this body did contain a spirit,
> A kingdom for it was too small a bound,
> But now two paces of the vilest earth
> Is room enough.
>
> (V.iv.88–91)

No matter how great one's life, one's honor can never outlast one's life, Harry states, since death reduces one to so little.

Henry's division of his forces at the very end of the final scene, as he announces his plan to send John and Westmoreland up to fight Northumberland and his own intent to take Harry to Wales to put down Glyndŵr, leaves the door wide open for the play's sequel, *2 Henry IV*, in which these dangling plot threads are resolved. In many ways, *1 Henry IV* is a play without a conclusion. Critics often refer to the two Henry IV plays as a single play with ten acts; under that interpretation, the *real* play is now only half over.

Important Quotations Explained

1. Yea, there thou mak'st me sad and mak'st me sin
   In envy that my Lord Northumberland
   Should be the father to so blest a son—
   A son who is the theme of honour's tongue,
   Amongst a grove the very straightest plant,
   Who is sweet Fortune's minion and her pride—
   Whilst I, by looking on the praise of him
   See riot and dishonor stain the brow
   Of my young Harry. O, that it could be proved
   That some night-tripping fairy had exchanged
   In cradle clothes our children where they lay,
   And called mine Percy, his Plantagenet!
                              (I.i.77–88)

These lines, which King Henry speaks in the first scene of the play,
set the stage for the conflict between Prince Harry and Hotspur.
Henry describes the fame and fortune of young Hotspur (the son of
"my Lord Northumberland"), calling him "the theme of honour's
tongue"; in comparison, he says, Prince Harry ("my young Harry")
has been sullied by "riot and dishonour." He then refers to an old
English folk superstition—one of the many references to folk culture
and magic in the play—about fairies who switched young children
at birth. Henry *wishes* that a fairy had switched Harry and Hotspur
at birth, so that Hotspur were really his son and Harry the son of
Northumberland. This quote is important for a number of reasons.
It foreshadows the rivalry of Harry and Hotspur, and it helps establish Henry's careworn, worried condition. Furthermore, it lets the
audience know that Harry is generally considered a disappointment,
and, by presenting both Harry and Hotspur as potential son figures
for Henry, it inaugurates the motif of doubles in the play.

2. I know you all, and will awhile uphold
    The unyoked humour of your idleness.
    Yet herein will I imitate the sun,
    Who doth permit the base contagious clouds
    To smother up his beauty from the world,
    That when he please again to be himself,
    Being wanted, he may be more wondered at
    By breaking through the foul and ugly mists
    Of vapours that did seem to strangle him.
    If all the year were playing holidays,
    To sport would be as tedious as to work;
    But when they seldom come, they wished-for come,
    And nothing pleaseth but rare accidents.
    So, when this loose behaviour I throw off
    And pay the debt I never promisèd,
    By how much better than my word I am,
    By so much shall I falsify men's hopes;
    And like bright metal on a sullen ground,
    My reformation, glitt'ring o'er my fault,
    Shall show more goodly and attract more eyes
    Than that which hath no foil to set it off.
    I'll so offend to make offence a skill,
    Redeeming time when men think least I will.
                                    (I.ii.173–195)

Prince Harry addresses this monologue to Falstaff and his friends, even though they have just left the room, leaving Harry all alone. It is in this speech that Harry first reveals his deception. His idling with the Boar's Head company is all an act, and when the need arises, he will cast off the act and reveal his true noble nature. Harry tells the departed Falstaff that he "will a while uphold / The unyoked humour of your idleness," but that, just as the sun permits itself to be covered by clouds so that the people who miss its light will be all the happier when it reappears, he too will eventually emerge from the cloud cover of his lower-class friends. Harry says that people quickly grow used to and tire of anything that is famil- iar: if every day were a holiday, he says, then holidays would seem as tiresome as work, because "nothing pleaseth but rare accidents."

Therefore, Harry concludes that by earning the people's disap- proval with his current behavior, he sets himself up to appear all the more glorious when he finally decides to earn their approval, since they will not take his high merit for granted. This quote is extremely important to the play, because it establishes the dramatic irony of Harry's character, known to no one but the audience and the prince himself. It also exposes the complexities and ambiguities of Harry's mind, showing an apparently virtuous young man who can manipulate and lie to others to achieve his somewhat selfish, albeit important, goals.

3. When I was dry with rage and extreme toil,
    . . .
    Came there a certain lord, neat and trimly dressed,
    Fresh as a bridegroom, and his chin, new-reaped
    Showed like a stubble-land at harvest-home.
    He was perfumèd like a milliner,
    . . .
    With many holiday and lady terms
    He questioned me; amongst the rest demanded
    My prisoners in your majesty's behalf.
    I then, all smarting with my wounds being cold —
    To be so pestered with a popinjay! —
    Out of my grief and my impatience
    Answered neglectingly, I know not what —
    He should, or should not — for he made me mad
    To see him shine so brisk, and smell so sweet,
    And talk so like a waiting gentlewoman
    . . .
    So cowardly, and but for these vile guns
    He would himself have been a soldier.
                              (I.iii.28–68)

Hotspur gives this speech to Henry to explain why he did not release a group of prisoners when ordered to do so by Henry's messenger. (The conflict over this group of prisoners is what precipitates the Percys' break from Henry in Act I.) Hotspur says that this messenger confronted him immediately after a pitched battle and that the man was so simpering and effeminate that it disgusted him. The speech is important because of the early insight it offers into Hotspur's character. He is a soldier through and through and has no patience for weakness, fashion, cowardice, manners, or the niceties of courtly behavior. It is highly ironic that Hotspur's speech about the messenger is so long and elaborate, because Hotspur takes such pains to portray himself as a man of action rather than words. Hotspur's description of his encounter with this man, on the other hand, is remarkably vivid and eloquent. Shakespeare achieves much through Hotspur's detailed account of the "neat and trimly dressed" courtier, who talks in "holiday and lady terms" and reminds Hotspur of a "popinjay" and a "waiting gentlewoman." Hotspur's disgust reaches its height when the courtier says that he too would have become a soldier "but for these vile guns." Thus, Shakespeare creates an amusing and believable character, the courtier, who never appears onstage, and also firmly establishes Hotspur's aggressive, masculine nature.

4.   FALSTAFF: But to say I know more harm in him than
     in myself were to say more than I know. That he is
     old, the more the pity, his white hairs do witness it.
     But that he is, saving your reverence, a whoremaster,
     that I utterly deny. If sack and sugar be a fault, God
     help the wicked. If to be old and merry be a sin, then
     many an old host that I know is damned. If to be fat
     be to be hated, then Pharaoh's lean kine are to be
     loved. No, my good lord, banish Peto, banish
     Bardolph, banish Poins, but for sweet Jack Falstaff,
     kind Jack Falstaff, true Jack Falstaff, valiant Jack
     Falstaff, and therefore more valiant being, as he is,

          old Jack Falstaff,
     Banish not him thy Harry's company,
     Banish not him thy Harry's company.
     Banish plump Jack, and banish all the world.

     PRINCE: I do; I will.
                              (II.v.425–439)

This exchange occurs during Harry and Falstaff's game of role-playing, as Falstaff pretends to be Harry so that Harry can prepare for his upcoming meeting with his father. Falstaff uses his time in the role of King Henry mainly to praise himself, urging Harry to keep Falstaff near him—something that the real king would never do, but certainly in keeping with Falstaff's character. Playing Harry, Falstaff lists his own faults, and then excuses each of them—"If sack and sugar be a fault, God help the wicked. If to be old and merry be a sin, then many and old host that I know is damned"—and then, improbably, begins to list his own supposed virtues, calling himself "sweet," "kind," "true," and "valiant." Falstaff is not sweet, kind, true, or valiant, but his constant claims to be these things are part of what makes him endearing. In any case, this speech is important because it lets us in on some of the complexities of Harry and Falstaff's relationship. Falstaff understands that he is undesirable company for Harry and worries that Harry will one day break his ties with him. So, in the role of King Henry, Falstaff urges Harry not to do so. Harry's icy reply, "I do; I will," foreshadows the moment of the actual break in the next play, 2 *Henry IV.*

5.   Well, 'tis no matter; honour pricks me on. Yea, but
      how if honour prick me off when I come on? How
      then? Can honour set-to a leg? No. Or an arm? No.
      Or take away the grief of a wound? No. Honour hath
      no skill in surgery, then? No. What is honour? A
      word. What is in that word "honour"? What is that
      "honour"? Air. A trim reckoning! Who hath it? He
      that died o' Wednesday. Doth he feel it? No. Doth he
      hear it? No. 'Tis insensible then? Yea, to the dead. But
      will it not live with the living? No. Why? Detraction
      will not suffer it. Therefore I'll none of it. Honour is a
      mere scutcheon. And so ends my catechism.
                              (V.i.129–139)

Falstaff delivers this diatribe against honor during the battle at Shrewsbury, just before the climax of the play. Linking honor to violence, Falstaff, who is about to go into battle, says that honor "pricks him on" to fight, meaning that honor motivates him; he then asks what he will do if honor "pricks him off," that is, kills or injures him. He says that honor is useless when one is wounded: it cannot set an arm or a leg, or take away the "grief of a wound," and it has "no skill in surgery." In fact, being merely a word, honor is nothing but thin air—that is, the breath that one exhales in saying a word. He says that the only people who have honor are the dead, and it does them no good, for they cannot feel or hear it. Furthermore, honor doesn't "live with the living" because honor is gained through death. Falstaff therefore concludes that honor is worthless, "a mere scutcheon," and that he wants nothing to do with it. In a play obsessed with the idea of honor, this speech comes out of

QUOTATIONS

nowhere to call into question the entire set of moral values on which most of the characters base their lives. It is one of the remarkable aspects of Falstaff's character that he is able to live so far outside the normal mores and expectations of his society; this speech epitomizes Falstaff's independent streak.

KEY FACTS

FULL TITLE
The History of Henry the Fourth (1 Henry IV)

AUTHOR
William Shakespeare

TYPE OF WORK
Play

GENRE
Historical drama, military drama

LANGUAGE
English

TIME AND PLACE WRITTEN
Probably 1596–1597, London

DATE OF FIRST PUBLICATION
1598 (in quarto), 1623 (in folio)

TONE
The tone of the play alternates between very serious drama and rollicking comedy. The drama is grave and ominous, and is centered on the careworn figure of King Henry IV and the rebellion of the Percys. The comedy is fast-paced, rambunctious, and punning, and centers around the character of Falstaff and the other rogues at the Boar's Head Tavern.

SETTING (TIME)
Around 1402–1403

SETTING (PLACE)
London, especially the royal palace and the Boar's Head Tavern; various other locales around England, including the battlefield of Shrewsbury, where the final act takes place

PROTAGONIST
Prince Harry

MAJOR CONFLICT

The Percy family, encouraged by the hot temper of the young nobleman Hotspur, seeks to overthrow the reigning king of England, Henry IV. Simultaneously, Harry, the crown prince of England, must work to win back his honor and his place in his father's esteem after squandering it by spending too much time with the rogue Falstaff and other unsuitable companions.

RISING ACTION

The king's confrontation with Hotspur; the robbery; the king's confrontation with Harry; the Percys' battle preparations

CLIMAX

The Battle of Shrewsbury in Act V, specifically Harry's duel with Hotspur

FALLING ACTION

The king's strategizing after the battle, leading into the play's sequel, 2 *Henry IV*

THEMES

The nature of honor; the legitimacy of rulership; high and low language

MOTIFS

Doubles; British cultures; the multiplicity of language; magic

SYMBOLS

The play is not heavily symbolic, though various characters represent various traits: for example, Hotspur represents the ideal of honor as a product of glory on the battlefield, and Glyndŵr represents the folk magic of Wales.

FORESHADOWING

Hotspur's confrontation with the king; the king's claim that Hotspur has more honor than Harry; Harry and Falstaff's role-playing; the robbery; Hotspur's confrontation with Kate.

STUDY QUESTIONS & ESSAY TOPICS

STUDY QUESTIONS

1.   *1 Henry IV is in many ways a study of contrasting characters, including Harry, Hotspur, Falstaff, and King Henry. Does the play have a single protagonist or many characters of equal importance? Why is the play named after King Henry?*

The simplest answer is that the play is named after King Henry because he is the king; all of Shakespeare's history plays are named after the person sitting on the throne during the time that they take place. Moreover, the play is concerned with detailing, in broad strokes, the reign of King Henry IV. Henry, however, is not the main character, and his actions are generally secondary to the plot. *1 Henry IV* does not really revolve around a particular protagonist but instead makes its thematic arguments by exploring the contrasts between its four major and many minor characters. If a single major character must be chosen, the likeliest candidate is Harry, whose mind is most nearly at the center of the play's focus. Given, too, that Harry emerges in the next two plays as the heroic King Henry V, the most glorified figure in all of Shakespeare's histories, it is probably feasible to read *1 Henry IV*, at least in part, as a kind of prelude to Harry's more mature adventures.

2.   1 Henry IV *explores the qualities of a king and how a king
ought to bear himself in relation to other people. Consider
the various candidates for kingship in the play (King
Henry IV himself, Prince Harry, Hotspur) and discuss
what qualities the main contenders would bring to bear
on kingship. Do these qualities help the eventual winners
defeat the losers, or is it merely a question of luck?*

King Henry possesses a certain regal grace. He believes that by
remaining strong and keeping himself aloof from the common people, he will command respect and authority. By contrast, Prince
Harry has spent a great deal of his time fraternizing with commoners, both to lower the expectations he must face and to get to know
the mind of England's people for the time when he is their ruler.
Both Henry and Harry are intelligent and patient and able to detach
themselves from a situation in order to think a plan through. By
contrast, Hotspur is rash, crude, impatient, and violent. His main
qualities as a king would be his capacity for swift and decisive action
and his commitment to personal honor. Shakespeare certainly dis-
qualifies Hotspur from being a viable candidate for the throne by
portraying his inability to exercise diplomacy and his frequent
thoughtless mistakes and blunders. Henry and Harry, however,
both make impressive leaders—especially Harry, who later
becomes the greatest ruler in all of Shakespeare's histories.

3. *The play contains many instances of symmetry, in which
    scenes or even people seem to be slightly altered
    reflections of other scenes or people. Look for scenes
    where you think that a previous event is being repeated or
    transformed or for characters who are explicitly
    contrasted or compared. Which scenes or characters are
    these? Why might Shakespeare use this technique?*

There are innumerable instances of symmetry in the play, including
Hotspur's and his uncle's similar complaints about Henry IV in
Act IV, scene iii and Act V, scene i, respectively; the contrast
between Harry and Hotspur, who act as son figures to Henry IV; the
contrast between Henry and Falstaff, who act as father figures to
Harry; the set of high noblemen at the top of the play's social hier-
archy and the set of low commoners at the bottom of it; and so on.
Shakespeare uses this technique largely as an instrument of contrast,
whereby a single thematic idea can be explored from two opposed
perspectives, such as Harry and Hotspur's contrasting ideas of
honor.

QUESTIONS & ESSAYS

4.   1 Henry IV *mixes prose and poetry to an extraordinary
       degree. Consider the places in which the two modes occur
       in the play. Why did Shakespeare choose to write his play
       this way? Do you think that some of the characters
       "demand" to speak in prose or in poetry? How would the
       character of Falstaff, for instance, be different if he spoke
       in iambic pentameter or that of King Henry if he always
       spoke in prose? Can you see Harry's shifts from poetry to
       prose and back again as an indication of changes in his
       frame of mind, his environment, or his ambitions over the
       course of the play?*

The multiplicity and variety of the English language used throughout *1 Henry IV* is one of its most interesting motifs, and the prose/
poetry contrast is generally used as a technique to help Shakespeare
capture the broad range of dialogic style he has incorporated into
his play. In general, the play's fast-paced, rough-hewn prose is the
language of commoners, while its elegant, courtly poetry is the language of the nobility. If Falstaff spoke in iambic pentameter, he
would lose the sense of freewheeling vulgarity that clings to him,
and if the king were to speak in prose, he would lose his sense of
regal stateliness. Generally, Harry speaks in prose around his common friends and uses poetry increasingly as he makes the transition
into the regal prince of the play's conclusion.

SUGGESTED ESSAY TOPICS

1. Many critics see in *1 Henry IV* a complicated pattern of *displacement*. Hotspur displaces Harry in his father's eyes, for instance, and Harry must win back the place he has lost (by killing Hotspur). Similarly, Falstaff has displaced King Henry IV as Harry's father figure. What choices lead to these displacements? Why do you think Shakespeare created them? How (and why) are they resolved—if they are resolved?

2. Many critics have found Falstaff more fascinating than any other character in the play. The critic Harold Bloom, for instance, takes a cue from Hegel in claiming that Falstaff and Hamlet are Shakespeare's two most intelligent characters: they are, as Hegel claims, "free artists of themselves," self-aware beings who invent themselves through their own self-descriptions; in fact, they are "men made out of words." What do you think Bloom means by this? Consider the way in which Falstaff uses words, humor, and punning not only to negotiate the world around him, but also to constantly describe and redescribe himself. What is the impression of Falstaff that we ultimately come away with, and where (or with whom) does it originate?

3. Think about Act II, scene iv, in which Hotspur is confronted by his wife about his plans for the rebellion. What does this scene tell us about Hotspur's character? What does it tell us about Renaissance marriage and the role of women in general? How does Shakespeare connect this analysis to the forward motion of his plot?

Review & Resources

Quiz

1. At what tavern do Falstaff and friends congregate?

   A. The Boar's Head
   B. The Sow's Ear
   C. The Pearl & Swine
   D. The Ford of Sevens

2. Where does the final battle of the play take place?

   A. Falkirk
   B. Yorktown
   C. Shrewsbury
   D. Shropshire

3. Who was king before Henry IV?

   A. Richard III
   B. Richard II
   C. Henry III
   D. Edward III

4. Why does Harry say he is spending so much time with Falstaff?

   A. To learn the old man's secrets of thievery
   B. To escape his father, whom he hates
   C. To trick Hotspur into thinking that he is a drunkard
   D. To lower expectations, so that when he chooses to act kingly, he will impress everyone all the more

5. Why does Kate confront Hotspur?

    A. He has not eaten well, slept well, or made love to her for two weeks

    B. He is plotting against her secret lover, Prince Harry

    C. He is having an affair with Mistress Quickly

    D. He prefers his horses to her

6. How do the Percys justify their rebellion?

    A. They say that Henry is a cruel and sadistic king

    B. They say that Henry has wasted the wealth of England fighting the Saracens

    C. They say that Henry attained the throne through witchcraft

    D. They say that Henry is ungrateful for the role they played in helping him seize the throne

7. In the battle, what does Falstaff carry in place of a pistol?

    A. A dagger

    B. A skin of wine

    C. A purse full of gold to bribe his enemies

    D. Nothing

8. Who kills Hotspur?

    A. Kate

    B. Falstaff

    C. King Henry

    D. Harry

9. Why does Henry decide to execute Worcester?

    A. He deviously chose not to convey Henry's peace offering to Hotspur

    B. He stole Henry's daughter and held her for ransom

    C. He is in league with France to overthrow England

    D. He is a Saracen

REVIEW & RESOURCES

10. Approximately when was the play written?

    A. 1564
    B. 1582
    C. 1596
    D. 1612

11. What is Glyndŵr's nationality?

    A. Irish
    B. Welsh
    C. Scottish
    D. Saxon

12. What is the Douglas's nationality?

    A. English
    B. Welsh
    C. French
    D. Scottish

13. To what family does Hotspur belong?

    A. Percy
    B. Woodville
    C. Lancaster
    D. Plantagenet

14. Who is John of Lancaster?

    A. Harry's older brother
    B. Harry's brother-in-law
    C. Harry's younger brother
    D. Harry's nephew

15. With whom does Harry trick Falstaff during the robbery?

    A. Hotspur
    B. Poins
    C. Bardolph
    D. Gadshill

16. Where did Gadshill get his name?

    A. From a church
    B. From a theater poster
    C. From the queen herself
    D. From a place where he has staged many robberies

17. How does Falstaff survive the battle?

    A. By fighting fiercely
    B. By playing dead
    C. By hiding underwater
    D. By fleeing to France

18. What is Falstaff's favorite literary device?

    A. The mixed metaphor
    B. The metonym
    C. The pun
    D. Prosopopoeia

19. What is Falstaff's first name?

    A. John
    B. James
    C. Joseph
    D. Jasper

20. Which captive does Hotspur wish to have released?

    A. Bolingbroke
    B. York
    C. Edmund of Norville
    D. Mortimer

21. How does the Archbishop of York feel about the king?

    A. He loves him as a brother
    B. He tolerates him, but only because Henry's reign is so profitable to the church
    C. He pretends to love him while secretly hoping for the rebels to defeat him
    D. He is an active participant in the rebellion against the king

22. Why does Hotspur's father say he will not go to battle?

    A. It cannot be won
    B. He is too sick
    C. He is wracked with grief over his wife's suicide
    D. He has recently discovered that Henry is his cousin

23. How did Henry obtain the crown?

    A. He inherited it from his father
    B. He won it in a jousting tournament
    C. He took it in a revolution
    D. He was given it by the Archbishop of Canterbury after the death of Lord Hastings

24. Which of the following traits do Harry and Hotspur have in common?

    A. Age
    B. Love for Kate
    C. Quick temper
    D. Sexual promiscuity

25. Who kills Falstaff?

    A. Harry
    B. Hotspur
    C. The Douglas
    D. Falstaff does not die in the play

SUGGESTIONS FOR FURTHER READING

BECKER, GEORGE J. *Shakespeare's Histories.* New York: Frederick Ungar, 1977.

BLOOM, HAROLD. *Shakespeare: The Invention of the Human.* New York: Riverhead Books, 1998.

BORIS, EDNA Z. *Shakespeare's English Kings: The People and the Law.* Rutherford, New Jersey: Fairleigh Dickinson University Press, 1978.

COUNCIL, NORMAN. *When Honour's at the Stake: Ideas of Honour in Shakespeare's History Plays.* New York: Barnes & Noble, 1973.

DESAI, R. W. *Falstaff: A Study of His Role in Shakespeare's History Plays.* India: Doaba House, 1976.

SHALVI, ALICE. *The Relationship of Renaissance Concepts of Honour to Shakespeare's Problem Plays.* Salzburg, Austria: University of Salzburg, 1972.

WATSON, ROBERT N. *Shakespeare and the Hazards of Ambition.* Cambridge: Harvard University Press, 1984.

A Note on the Type

The typeface used in SparkNotes study guides is Sabon, created by master typographer Jan Tschichold in 1964. Tschichold revolutionized the field of graphic design twice: first with his use of asymmetrical layouts and sanserif type in the 1930s when he was affiliated with the Bauhaus, then by abandoning assymetry and calling for a return to the classic ideals of design. Sabon, his only extant typeface, is emblematic of his latter program: Tschichold's design is a recreation of the types made by Claude Garamond, the great French typographer of the Renaissance, and his contemporary Robert Granjon. Fittingly, it is named for Garamond's apprentice, Jacques Sabon.

SPARKNOTES
TEST PREPARATION
GUIDES

The SparkNotes team figured it was time to cut standardized tests down to size. We've studied the tests for you, so that SparkNotes test prep guides are:

Smarter
Packed with critical-thinking skills and test-
taking strategies that will improve your score.

Better
Fully up to date, covering all new features of the tests,
with study tips on every type of question.

Faster
Our books cover exactly what you need to
know for the test. No more, no less.

SparkNotes Guide to the SAT & PSAT
SparkNotes Guide to the SAT & PSAT — Deluxe Internet Edition
SparkNotes Guide to the ACT
SparkNotes Guide to the ACT — Deluxe Internet Edition
SparkNotes SAT Verbal Workbook
SparkNotes SAT Math Workbook
SparkNotes Guide to the SAT II Writing
5 More Practice Tests for the SAT II Writing
SparkNotes Guide to the SAT II U.S. History
5 More Practice Tests for the SAT II History
SparkNotes Guide to the SAT II Math Ic
5 More Practice Tests for the SAT II Math Ic
SparkNotes Guide to the SAT II Math IIc
5 More Practice Tests for the SAT II Math IIc
SparkNotes Guide to the SAT II Biology
5 More Practice Tests for the SAT II Biology
SparkNotes Guide to the SAT II Physics

SparkNotes™ Literature Guides